CYPHERPUNKS

JULIAN ASSANGE

CYPHERPUNKS

FREEDOM *AND THE* FUTURE
OF THE INTERNET

JULIAN
ASSANGE

with JACOB APPELBAUM

ANDY MÜLLER-MAGUHN

and JÉRÉMIE ZIMMERMANN

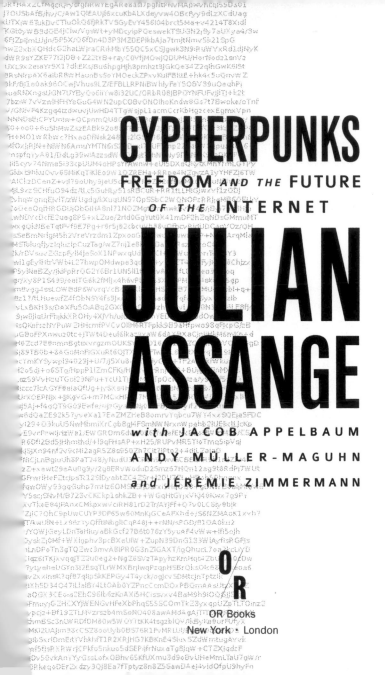

OR Books
New York · London

© 2012 Julian Assange

Published by OR Books, New York and London
Visit our website at www.orbooks.com

First printing 2012

Cataloging-in-Publication data is available from the Library of Congress.
A catalog record for this book is available from the British Library.

ISBN 978-1-939293-00-8 paperback
ISBN 978-1-939293-01-5 e-book

This book is set in the typeface Minion.
Typeset by Lapiz Digital, Chennai, India.
Printed by BookMobile in the United States and CPI Books Ltd in the United
Kingdom. The U.S. printed edition of this book comes on Forest Stewardship
Council-certified, 30% recycled paper. The printer, BookMobile, is 100%
wind-powered.

WHAT IS A CYPHERPUNK?

Cypherpunks advocate for the use of cryptography and similar methods as ways to achieve societal and political change.[1] Founded in the early 1990s, the movement has been most active during the 1990s "cryptowars" and following the 2011 internet spring. The term *cypherpunk*, derived from (cryptographic) *cipher* and *punk*, was added to the Oxford English Dictionary in 2006.[2]

CONTENTS

INTRODUCTION: A CALL TO CRYPTOGRAPHIC ARMS

This book is not a manifesto. There is not time for that. This book is a warning.

The world is not sliding, but galloping into a new transnational dystopia. This development has not been properly recognized outside of national security circles. It has been hidden by secrecy, complexity and scale. The internet, our greatest tool of emancipation, has been transformed into the most dangerous facilitator of totalitarianism we have ever seen. The internet is a threat to human civilization.

These transformations have come about silently, because those who know what is going on work in the global surveillance industry and have no incentives to speak out. Left to its own trajectory, within a few years, global civilization will be a postmodern surveillance dystopia, from which escape for all but the most skilled individuals will be impossible. In fact, we may already be there.

While many writers have considered what the internet means for global civilization, they are wrong. They are wrong because they do not have the sense of perspective that direct experience brings. They are wrong because they have never met the enemy.

No description of the world survives first contact with the enemy.

We have met the enemy.

Over the last six years WikiLeaks has had conflicts with nearly every powerful state. We know the new surveillance state from an insider's perspective, because we have plumbed its secrets. We know it from a combatant's perspective, because we have had to protect our people, our finances and our sources from it. We know it from a global perspective, because we have people, assets and information in nearly every country. We know it from the perspective of time, because we have been fighting this phenomenon for years and have seen it double and spread, again and again. It is an invasive parasite, growing fat off societies that merge with the internet. It is rolling over the planet, infecting all states and peoples before it.

What is to be done?

Once upon a time in a place that was neither here nor there, we, the constructors and citizens of the young internet discussed the future of our new world.

We saw that the relationships between all people would be mediated by our new world, and that the nature of states, which are defined by how people exchange information, economic value, and force, would also change.

We saw that the merger between existing state structures and the internet created an opening to change the nature of states.

First, recall that states are systems through which coercive force flows. Factions within a state may compete for support, leading to democratic surface phenomena, but the underpinnings of states are the systematic application, and avoidance, of violence. Land ownership, property, rents, dividends, taxation, court fines, censorship, copyrights and trademarks are all enforced by the threatened application of state violence.

Most of the time we are not even aware of how close to violence we are, because we all grant concessions to avoid it. Like sailors smelling the breeze, we rarely contemplate how our surface world is propped up from below by darkness.

In the new space of the internet what would be the mediator of coercive force?

Does it even make sense to ask this question? In this otherworldly space, this seemingly platonic realm of ideas and information flow, could there be a notion of coercive force? A force that could modify historical records, tap phones, separate people, transform complexity into rubble, and erect walls, like an occupying army?

The platonic nature of the internet, ideas and information flows, is debased by its physical origins. Its foundations are fiber optic cable lines stretching across the ocean floors, satellites spinning above our heads, computer servers housed in buildings in cities from New York to Nairobi. Like the soldier who slew Archimedes with a mere sword, so too could an armed militia take control of the peak development of Western civilization, our platonic realm.

The new world of the internet, abstracted from the old world of brute atoms, longed for independence. But states and their friends moved to control our new world—by controlling its physical underpinnings. The state, like an army around an oil well, or a customs agent extracting bribes at the border, would soon learn to leverage its control of physical space to gain control over our platonic realm. It would prevent the independence we had dreamed of, and then, squatting on fiber optic lines and around satellite ground stations, it would go on to mass intercept the information flow of our new world—its very essence—even as every human, economic, and political relationship embraced it. The state would leech into the veins and arteries of our new societies, gobbling up every relationship expressed or communicated, every web page read, every message sent and every thought googled, and then store this knowledge, billions of interceptions a day, undreamed of power, in vast top secret warehouses, forever. It would go on to mine and mine again this treasure, the collective private intellectual output of humanity, with ever more sophisticated search and pattern finding algorithms, enriching the treasure and maximizing the power imbalance between interceptors and the world of interceptees. And then the state would reflect what it had learned back into the physical world, to start wars, to target drones, to manipulate UN committees and trade deals, and to do favors for its vast connected network of industries, insiders and cronies.

But we discovered something. Our one hope against total domination. A hope that with courage, insight and solidarity we could use to resist. A strange property of the physical universe that we live in.

The universe believes in encryption.

It is easier to encrypt information than it is to decrypt it.

We saw we could use this strange property to create the laws of a new world. To abstract away our new platonic realm from its base underpinnings of satellites, undersea cables and their controllers. To fortify our space behind a cryptographic veil. To create new lands barred to those who control physical reality, because to follow us into them would require infinite resources.

And in this manner to declare independence.

Scientists in the Manhattan Project discovered that the universe permitted the construction of a nuclear bomb. This was not an obvious conclusion. Perhaps nuclear weapons were not within the laws of physics. However, the universe believes in atomic bombs and nuclear reactors. They are a phenomenon the universe blesses, like salt, sea or stars.

Similarly, the universe, our physical universe, has that property that makes it possible for an individual or a group of individuals to reliably, automatically, even without knowing, encipher something, so that all the resources and all the political will of the strongest superpower on earth may not decipher it. And the paths of encipherment between people can mesh together to create regions free from the coercive force of the outer state. Free from mass interception. Free from state control.

In this way, people can oppose their will to that of a fully mobilized superpower and win. Encryption is an embodiment of the laws of physics, and it does not listen to the bluster of states, even transnational surveillance dystopias.

It isn't obvious that the world had to work this way. But somehow the universe smiles on encryption.

Cryptography is the ultimate form of non-violent direct action.

While nuclear weapons states can exert unlimited violence over even millions of individuals, strong cryptography means that a state, even by exercising unlimited violence, cannot violate the intent of individuals to keep secrets from them.

Strong cryptography can resist an unlimited application of violence. No amount of coercive force will ever solve a math problem.

But could we take this strange fact about the world and build it up to be a basic emancipatory building block for the independence of mankind in the platonic realm of the internet? And as societies merged with the internet could that liberty then be reflected back into physical reality to redefine the state?

Recall that states are the systems which determine where and how coercive force is consistently applied.

The question of how much coercive force can seep into the platonic realm of the internet from the physical world is answered by cryptography and the cypherpunks' ideals.

As states merge with the internet and the future of our civilization becomes the future of the internet, we must redefine force relations.

If we do not, the universality of the internet will merge global humanity into one giant grid of mass surveillance and mass control.

We must raise an alarm. This book is a watchman's shout in the night.

On March 20, 2012, while under house arrest in the United Kingdom awaiting extradition, I met with three friends and fellow watchmen on the principle that perhaps in unison our voices can wake up the town. We must communicate what we have learned while there is still a chance for you, the reader, to understand and act on what is happening.

It is time to take up the arms of our new world, to fight for ourselves and for those we love.

Our task is to secure self-determination where we can, to hold back the coming dystopia where we cannot, and if all else fails, to accelerate its self-destruction.

—Julian Assange, London, October 2012

DISCUSSION PARTICIPANTS

JULIAN ASSANGE is the editor in chief of and visionary behind WikiLeaks.[3] An original contributor to the Cypherpunk mailing list, Julian is now one of the most prominent exponents of cypherpunk philosophy in the world. His work with WikiLeaks has given political currency to the traditional cypherpunk juxtaposition: "privacy for the weak, transparency for the powerful." While his most visible work involves robust exercise of the freedom of expression to force transparency and accountability on powerful institutions, he is also an incisive critic of state and corporate encroachment upon the privacy of individuals. Julian is the author of numerous software projects in line with the cypherpunk philosophy, such as the first TCP/IP port scanner strobe.c, the rubberhose deniable encryption file system, and the original code for WikiLeaks.[4] In his teens Julian was an early computer and network security researcher, before some kinds of hacking were defined in law as criminal activity. Subsequently an activist and internet service provider to Australia during the 1990s, Julian has also co-written a history of the international hacker movement with Sulette Dreyfus, titled *Underground*, upon which the movie *Underground: The Julian Assange Story* was loosely based.[5]

JACOB APPELBAUM is a founder of Noisebridge in San Francisco, a member of the Berlin Chaos Computer Club and a developer.[6] Jacob is an advocate and a researcher for the Tor Project, which is an online anonymity system for all people to resist surveillance and to circumvent internet censorship.[7] His focus for the last decade has been helping environmental and human rights activists. Toward this goal he has published novel security, privacy and anonymity-related research in a number of areas from computer forensics to medical marijuana. Jacob believes that everybody has the right to read, without restriction, and the right to speak freely, with no exception. In 2010, when Julian Assange could not deliver a talk in New York, Jacob gave the talk instead. Since then he, his friends and his family have been harassed by the United States government: interrogated at airports, subjected to invasive pat-downs while being threatened with implied impending prison rape by law enforcement officials, had his equipment confiscated and his online services subject to secret subpoena. Jacob is uncowed by these measures, continues to fight ongoing legal issues, and remains an outspoken advocate of freedom of expression, and a vocal supporter of WikiLeaks.

ANDY MÜLLER-MAGUHN is a long-time member of the Chaos Computer Club in Germany, former board member and spokesman.[8] He is one of the co-founders of EDRI, European Digital Rights, an NGO for the enforcement of human rights in the digital age.[9] From 2000 to 2003 he was elected by European internet users to be the European Director of ICANN, the Internet Corporation for Assigned Names and Numbers, which is responsible for worldwide policies for how the "names and numbers" of the internet should run.[10] He is a specialist on telecommunication and other surveillance, working in a journalistic capacity on the surveillance industry with his project wiki, buggedplanet.info.[11] Andy works in cryptographic communications and created with others a company called Cryptophone, which markets secure voice communication devices to commercial clients and is providing strategic consultancy in the context of network architecture.[12]

JÉRÉMIE ZIMMERMANN is the co-founder and spokesperson for the citizen advocacy group La Quadrature du Net, the most prominent European organization defending anonymity rights online and promoting awareness of regulatory attacks on online freedoms.[13] Jérémie works to build tools for the public to use to take part in public debate and to try to change things. He is mostly involved with the copyright wars, the debate around net neutrality and other regulatory issues that are crucial for the future of a free internet. Recently, his group La Quadrature du Net had a historic success in European politics, successfully marshaling a public campaign to defeat the Anti-Counterfeit and Trade Agreement (ACTA) in the European Parliament. Shortly after participating in the discussion that forms the basis of this book, Jérémie was stopped by two FBI officers while leaving the United States, and was interrogated about WikiLeaks.

EDITOR'S NOTE

To increase *Cypherpunks'* accessibility to a general reader, each of the participants in the original discussion was given an opportunity to substantially expand on, clarify and footnote their points. The order of the edited manuscript in general adheres to the dynamic of the original discussion.

NOTE ON THE VARIOUS ATTEMPTS TO PERSECUTE WIKILEAKS AND PEOPLE ASSOCIATED WITH IT

At several points in the following discussion references are made to recent events in the story of WikiLeaks and its publishing efforts. These may be obscure to readers unfamiliar with the story of WikiLeaks, so they are summarized here at the outset.

It is WikiLeaks' mission to receive information from whistleblowers, release it to the public, and then defend against the inevitable legal and political attacks. It is a routine occurrence for powerful states and organizations to attempt to suppress WikiLeaks publications, and as the publisher of last resort this is one of the hardships WikiLeaks was built to endure.

In 2010 WikiLeaks engaged in its most famous publications to date, revealing systematic abuse of official secrecy within the US military and government. These publications are known as Collateral Murder, the War Logs, and Cablegate.[14] The response has been a concerted and ongoing effort to destroy WikiLeaks by the US government and its allies.

THE WIKILEAKS GRAND JURY
As a direct consequence of WikiLeaks' publications the US government launched a multi-agency criminal investigation into Julian

Assange and WikiLeaks staff, supporters and alleged associates. A Grand Jury was convened in Alexandria, Virginia, with the support of the Department of Justice and the FBI to look into the possibility of bringing charges, including conspiracy charges under the Espionage Act 1917, against Julian Assange and others. US officials have said that the investigation is of "unprecedented scale and nature." In Grand Jury proceedings no judge or defense counsel is present. Congressional committee hearings have since heard the suggestion from members of the US Congress that the Espionage Act could be used as a tool to target journalists who "knowingly publish leaked information," suggesting that the approach is being normalized in the US justice system.[15]

At the date of publication, the WikiLeaks investigation continues.[16] Several people have been legally compelled to give evidence. Court proceedings in the trial of Bradley Manning, the soldier accused of passing information to WikiLeaks, reveal an FBI file on the investigation of WikiLeaks that runs to over 42,100 pages, some 8,000 of which refer to Manning. Bradley Manning has been detained without trial for over 880 days. UN Special Rapporteur for Torture, Juan Mendez, formally found that Bradley Manning had been treated in a manner which was cruel and inhuman, and which possibly amounted to torture.[17]

CALLS FOR THE ASSASSINATION OF JULIAN ASSANGE AND PUBLICLY DECLARED WIKILEAKS TASK FORCES

The Grand Jury investigation is not the only avenue of attack on WikiLeaks. In December 2010, in the wake of Cablegate, various active US politicians called for the extrajudicial assassination of Julian Assange, including by drone strike. US senators labeled WikiLeaks a "terrorist organization" and named Assange a "high-tech terrorist" and an "enemy combatant" engaged in "cyber warfare."[18]

A 120-strong US Pentagon team called the WikiLeaks Task Force, or WTF, was set up ahead of the release of the Iraq War Logs and Cablegate, dedicated to "taking action" against WikiLeaks. Similar publicly declared task forces in the FBI, the CIA and the US State Department are also still in operation.[19]

DIRECT CENSORSHIP

In an act of unprecedented censorship of a journalistic publication, the US government pressured internet service providers to cease services to WikiLeaks.org. On December 1, 2010 Amazon removed WikiLeaks from its storage servers, and on December 2 the DNS service pointing to the Wikileaks.org domain was disrupted. WikiLeaks was kept online during this period as the result of a "mass-mirroring" effort, whereby thousands of supporters of WikiLeaks copied the website, and hosted their own version, distributing the IP addresses through social networks.[20]

The Obama administration warned federal employees that materials released by WikiLeaks remained classified—even though they were being published by some of the world's leading news organizations including the *New York Times* and the *Guardian*. Employees were told that accessing the material, whether on WikiLeaks.org or in the *New York Times*, would amount to a security violation.[21] Government agencies such as the Library of Congress, the Commerce Department and the US military blocked access to WikiLeaks materials over their networks. The ban was not limited to the public sector. Employees from the US government warned academic institutions that students hoping to pursue a career in public service should stay clear of material released by WikiLeaks in their research and in their online activity.

FINANCIAL CENSORSHIP: THE BANKING BLOCKADE

WikiLeaks is funded by donations from supporters. In December 2010 major banking and financial institutions, including VISA, MasterCard, PayPal and Bank of America, bowed to unofficial US pressure and began to deny financial services to WikiLeaks. They blocked bank transfers and all donations made with major credit cards. While these are American institutions, their ubiquity in world finance meant that willing donors in both America and around the world were denied the option of sending money to WikiLeaks to support its publishing activities.

The "banking blockade," as it has become known, is being conducted outside of any judicial or administrative procedure and remains in place at the date of publication. WikiLeaks has been pursuing major court cases in different jurisdictions across the world in order to break the blockade, with some preliminary victories, and the legal processes are ongoing. In the meantime WikiLeaks has been denied income, has elevated costs, and has been operating on reserve funds for nearly two years.

The banking blockade is an assertion of the power to control financial transactions between third parties. It directly undermines the economic freedoms of individuals. Beyond even this, the existential threat it poses to WikiLeaks exemplifies a new and troubling form of global economic censorship. [22]

Some people allegedly associated with WikiLeaks, along with supporters and WikiLeaks staff themselves, have had mysterious issues with their bank accounts—from account details to full bank account closure.

HARASSMENT OF JACOB APPELBAUM AND JÉRÉMIE ZIMMERMANN

On July 17, 2010 Julian Assange was slated to speak at the HOPE hacker conference in New York City. He canceled, and Jacob Appelbaum appeared in his stead. Since this appearance law enforcement agencies have been running a campaign of harassment against Appelbaum and people in his life. Appelbaum has been routinely detained, searched, denied access to legal counsel and interrogated at border crossings whenever he travels into and out of the United States. His equipment has been seized and his rights violated, during which he has been threatened with further violations of his rights. His detainment and harassment has involved dozens of US agencies, from the Department for Homeland Security Immigration and Customs Enforcement to the US Army. These detentions even include the refusal of access to toilets as a method of pressuring compliance. Through all this, Appelbaum has never been charged or told by the government why he is being harassed.[23]

In mid-June 2011, while preparing to board a plane at Washington's Dulles Airport, Jérémie Zimmermann was stopped by two self-identified FBI agents. The agents questioned him about WikiLeaks and threatened him with arrest and imprisonment.

Appelbaum and Zimmermann are among a long list of friends, supporters, or alleged associates of Julian Assange who have been subject to harassment and surveillance by US agencies, a list that includes lawyers and journalists engaged in the course of their professional duties.

WARRANTLESS SEIZURE OF ELECTRONIC RECORDS AND THE "TWITTER SUBPOENA CASE"

On December 14, 2010 Twitter received an "administrative subpoena" from the US Department of Justice ordering it to give up information that might be relevant to an investigation into WikiLeaks. The subpoena was a so-called "2703(d) order," referring to a section of the Stored Communications Act. Under this law the US government claims the authority to compel the disclosure of private electronic communication records without the need for a judge to issue a search warrant—effectively getting around Fourth Amendment protections against arbitrary search and seizure.

The subpoena sought user names, correspondence records, addresses, telephone numbers, bank account details, and credit card numbers from accounts and people allegedly associated with WikiLeaks, including Jacob Appelbaum, Icelandic parliamentarian Birgitta Jonsdottir, Dutch businessman and internet pioneer Rop Gonggrijp, and WikiLeaks itself. Under the terms of the subpoena Twitter was gagged from even telling them of the existence of the order. However, Twitter successfully appealed against the gag clause and won the right to inform the targets that their records were being requested.

Having been told about the subpoena by Twitter, on January 26, 2011 Appelbaum, Jonsdottir and Gonggrijp, represented by Kecker and Van Nest, the American Civil Liberties Union and the Electronic Frontier Foundation, had their attorneys jointly file a motion to vacate the order. This has become known as the "Twitter subpoena case."[24] A further motion was filed by Appelbaum's attorney requesting to unseal the still-secret court records of the government's attempts to collect his private data from Twitter and any other companies. Both motions were denied by a US Magistrate Judge on March 11, 2011. The plaintiffs appealed.

On October 9, 2011 the *Wall Street Journal* revealed that the Californian email provider Sonic.net had also received a subpoena demanding the data of Jacob Appelbaum. Sonic had fought the government order and lost, but had obtained permission to disclose that it had been forced to turn over Appelbaum's information. The *Wall Street Journal* also reported that Google had been served a similar subpoena, but did not say whether Google had challenged it in court.[25]

On November 10, 2011 a federal judge decided against Appelbaum, Jonsdottir and Gonggrijp, ruling that Twitter must give their information to the Justice Department.[26] On January 20, 2012 the plaintiffs again appealed, seeking to challenge the refusal to unseal orders that might have been sent to companies other than Twitter."[27] At the time of publication, the case is ongoing.

INCREASED COMMUNICATION VERSUS
INCREASED SURVEILLANCE

JULIAN: If we go back to this time in the early 1990s when you had the rise of the cypherpunk movement in response to state bans on cryptography, a lot of people were looking at the power of the internet to provide free uncensored communications compared to mainstream media. But the cypherpunks always saw that, in fact, combined with this was also the power to surveil all the communications that were occurring. We now have increased communication versus increased surveillance. Increased communication means you have extra freedom relative to the people who are trying to control ideas and manufacture consent, and increased surveillance means just the opposite.

The surveillance is far more evident now than it was when bulk surveillance was just being done by the Americans, the British, the Russians and some other governments like the Swiss and the French. Now it is being done by everyone, and by nearly every state, because of the commercialization of mass surveillance. And it's totalizing now, because people put all their political ideas, their family communications, and their friendships on to the internet. So it's not just that there is increased surveillance of the communication that was already there; it's that there is so much more communication. And it's not just an increase in the volume of communication; it's an increase in the types of communication. All these new types of communication that would previously have been private are now being mass intercepted.

There is a battle between the power of this information collected by insiders, these shadow states of information that are starting to develop, swapping with each other, developing connections with each other and with the private sector, versus the increased size of the commons with the internet as a common tool for humanity to speak to itself.

I want to think about how we present our ideas. The big problem I've had, as someone who is steeped in state surveillance and understanding how the transnational security industry has developed over the past twenty years, is that I'm too familiar with it and so I don't understand how to see this from a common perspective. But now our world is everyone's world, because everyone has thrown the inner core of their lives onto the internet. We have to somehow communicate what we know while we still can.

ANDY: I suggest not looking at it from a citizen's point of view but from the point of view of people in power. The other day I was at this strange conference in Washington and I met these guys with a German embassy badge. I approached them and I said, "Oh, you're from the German embassy," and they said, "Ah, not exactly from the embassy, we are from near Munich." It turned out they were from the foreign intelligence and I asked them at the evening buffet, "So, what is the focus of secrecy?" They told me, "Well, it's about slowing down processes in order to better control them." That's the core of this kind of intelligence work, to slow down a process by taking away the ability of people to understand it. To declare things secret means you limit the amount of people who have the knowledge and therefore the ability to affect the process.

If you look at the internet from the perspective of people in power then the last twenty years have been frightening. They see the internet like an illness that affects their ability to define reality, to define what is going on, which is then used to define what the people know of what is going on and their ability to interact with it. If you look at, say, Saudi Arabia, where by some historical accident religious leaders and the people owning the majority of the country are the same, their interest in change is in the zeros. Zero to minus five, maybe. They look at the internet like an illness and ask their consultants, "Do you have some medicine against this thing out there? We need to be immune if this affects our country, if this internet thingy comes." And the answer is mass surveillance. It is, "We need to control it totally, we need to filter, we need to know everything that they do." And that is what has happened in the last twenty years. There was massive investment in surveillance because people in power feared that the internet would affect their way of governance.

JULIAN: And yet despite this mass surveillance, mass communication has led to millions of people being able to come to a fast consensus. If you can go from a normal position to a new mass consensus position very quickly, then while the state might be able to see it developing, there's not enough time to formulate an effective response.

Now that said, there was a Facebook-organized protest in 2008 in Cairo. It did surprise the Mubarak government, and as a result these people were tracked down using Facebook.[28] In 2011, in a manual which was one of the most important documents used in the Egyptian revolution, the first page says "Do not use Twitter or Facebook" to distribute the manual, and the last page says "Do not use Twitter or Facebook" to distribute the manual.[29] Nonetheless, plenty of Egyptians did use Twitter and Facebook. But the reason they survived is because the revolution was successful. If it had not been successful, then those people would have been in a very, very grim position. And let's not forget that pretty early on President Mubarak cut off the internet in Egypt. It is actually questionable whether the internet blackout facilitated the revolution or harmed it. Some people think it facilitated it, because people had to go out on the street to get news about what was happening, and once you're out on the street you're out on the street. And people were directly affected because their cell phone and internet didn't work anymore.

So if it is going to be successful, there needs to be a critical mass, it needs to happen fast, and it needs to win, because if it doesn't win then that same infrastructure that allows a fast consensus to develop will be used to track down and marginalize all the people who were involved in seeding the consensus.

So that was Egypt, which, yes, was a US ally, but which is not a part of the English-speaking intelligence alliance of the US, the UK, Australia, New Zealand and Canada. Now instead let's try to imagine the Egyptian revolution kicking off in the United States—what would happen to Facebook and Twitter? They would be taken over by the state. And if the revolution was not successful they would be plumbed, as they are now, by the CIA and FBI for details on who were the critical participants.

JÉRÉMIE: It's difficult to disassociate surveillance from control. We need to address both. That's more my interest—the control of the internet, whether it is by governments or corporations.

JACOB: I think it's pretty clear that censorship is a by-product of surveillance generally speaking, whether it's self-censorship or actually technical censorship, and I think that an important way to convey this to regular people is to do it non-technically. For example, if we built roads the way that we build the internet, every road would have to have surveillance cameras and microphones that no one except the police could access, or someone who has successfully pretended to be the police.

JULIAN: They're getting there, Jake, in the UK.

JACOB: When you build a road it is not a requirement that every inch can be monitored with perfect surveillance that is only available to a secret group of people. Explaining to everyday people that that is the way we are building roads on the internet and then requiring people to use those roads—that is something that regular people can connect with when they realize that the original builders of the road will not always be the ones in control.

ANDY: But some people don't even build roads. They put a garden out there and invite everybody to be naked. So now we're talking Facebook! It's a business case to make people comfortable with disclosing their data.

JACOB: Right. People were compensated for being in the Stasi—the old East German state security—and they are compensated for participating in Facebook. It's just in Facebook they are compensated with social credits—to get laid by their neighbor—instead of being paid off directly. And it's important to just relate it to the human aspect, because it's not about technology, it's about control through surveillance. It's the perfect Panopticon in some ways.[30]

JULIAN: I'm quite interested in the philosophy of technique. Technique means not just a piece of technology but it means, say, majority consensus on a board, or the structure of a parliament—it's systematized interaction. For example, it seems to me that feudal systems came from the technique of mills. Once you had centralized mills, which required huge investments and which were easily subject to physical control, then it was quite natural that you would end up with feudal relations as a result. As time has gone by we seem to have developed increasingly sophisticated techniques. Some of these techniques can be democratized; they can be spread to everyone. But the majority of them—because of their complexity—are techniques that form as a result of strongly interconnected organizations like Intel Corporation. Perhaps the underlying tendency of technique is to go through these periods of discovering technique, centralizing technique, democratizing technique—when the knowledge about how to do it floods out in the next generation that is educated. But I think that the general tendency for technique is to centralize control in those people who control the physical resources of techniques.

Something like a semi-conductor manufacturer is, I think, the ultimate example of that, where you need such order that the air itself must be pure, where you need a construction plant that has thousands of people in it who have to wear hairnets to keep every little skin flake, every bit of hair away from the semi-conductor manufacturing process, which is a multi-step process that is extremely complicated. And there are literally millions of hours of research knowledge possessed by the semi-conductor manufacturing organization. If those things are popular, which they are, and they underpin the internet, then coded within internet liberation is semi-conductor manufacturing. And coded within semi-conductor manufacturing is the ability for whoever has physical control of the semi-conductor manufacturer to extract enormous concessions.

So underpinning the high-tech communications revolution—and the liberty that we have extracted from that—is the whole neoliberal, transnational, globalized modern market economy. It is in fact the peak of that. It is the height, in terms of technological achievement, that the modern globalized neoliberal economy can produce. The internet is underpinned by extremely complex trade interactions between optical fiber manufacturers, semi-conductor manufacturers, mining companies that dig all this stuff up, and all the financial lubricants to make the trade happen, courts to enforce private property laws and so on. So it really is the top of the pyramid of the whole neoliberal system.

ANDY: On the point about technique, when Johannes Gutenberg invented the printing press, it was actually forbidden occasionally in parts of Germany and that's the way it spread all over the country, because when it was forbidden in one area they moved to another jurisdiction.[31] I didn't study it in all the details but what I know is that they messed up with the Catholic Church because they were breaking the monopoly on printing books, and once they got into legal trouble they moved on to a place where it was not forbidden. In a way this helped to spread it.

The internet was, I think, slightly different because on the one hand you have machines that can be used as a production facility, which even the Commodore 64 was, in a way, as most people used it for other purposes.

JULIAN: So, each little machine that you had you could run your own software.

ANDY: Yes. And you could also use it to distribute ideas. But on the other hand, philosophically, as John Gilmore—one of the founders of the US based Electronic Frontier Foundation—said at the beginning of the 1990s when the internet attained global reach, "The Net interprets censorship as damage and routes around it."[32] As we know today, that was a mixture of technical interpretation combined with an optimistic impact view, a kind of wishful thinking and also a kind of self-fulfilling prophecy.

JULIAN: But it was true for Usenet, which is a many-to-many e-mail system, if you like, that started about thirty years ago. To explain Usenet simply, imagine there is no difference between people and servers and every person is running their own Usenet server. You write something, and you give it to one or two people. They (automatically) check to see if they already have it. If they don't already have it they take it and give it to everyone they are connected to. And so on. And as a result the message floods through everyone and everyone eventually gets a copy. If any person is engaged in censorship then they are just ignored, it doesn't make any difference. The message still spreads through all the people who are not censors. Gilmore was speaking about Usenet, he was not speaking about the internet. He was also not speaking about web pages.

ANDY: While this is technically correct, the interpretation of his words and their long-term impact was to generate people who understood themselves as the internet. People said, "Ok, there's censorship, we'll route around it," where the politician with no technical understanding thought, "Oh shit, there's a new technology that limits our control of the information sphere." So I think Gilmore, who was one of the fore-thinkers of cypherpunk, did a great job of leading things in this direction, which inspired the whole crypto-anarchistic way of having your own form of anonymous communication without fearing that you will be followed up.

JÉRÉMIE: I see a difference with what we describe as the spreading of technology, because in the case of the mill and the printing press you had to look at one to understand how it works, whereas now we are increasingly building control inside the technology. The control is built-in. If you look at a modern computer in most cases you cannot even open it to get to know all the components. And all the components are in small cases—you cannot know what they are doing.

ANDY: Because of the complexity?

JÉRÉMIE: Because of the complexity and also because the technology itself is not intended to be understood. That's the case with proprietary technology.[33] Cory Doctorow describes it in his "The War on General-Purpose Computing."[34] Where a computer is a generic machine, you can do everything with it. You can process any information as an input; transform it into anything as an output. And more and more we're building devices that are those general-purpose computers but which are restricted to do just GPS or just telephone or just MP3 player. More and more we are building machines that have built-in control, to forbid the user from doing certain things.

JULIAN: That's built-in control to prevent people understanding it and modifying it from the purpose that the manufacturer wanted it for, but we have worse than this now, because it is actually connected up to the network.

JÉRÉMIE: Yes, so it can contain the function to monitor the user and its data. This is why free software is so important for a free society.

ANDY: I totally agree that we need the general-purpose machine, but this morning when I was trying to fly here from Berlin the plane actually aborted starting—it's the first time this has happened to me. The plane drove to the side and the Captain said, "Ladies and gentlemen, we had a failure in the electrical systems so we decided to stop and restart the systems." I was actually thinking, "Oh shit, sounds like Windows reboot, Control Alt Delete—maybe it works!" So actually, I would not be totally unhappy to have a single-purpose machine on a plane which just does that and does that very well. If

I'm sitting in a flying machine I don't want the pilots to be distracted by playing Tetris or having Stuxnet or whatever.[35]

JÉRÉMIE: The plane by itself doesn't process your personal data, it doesn't have control over your life.

ANDY: Well, a flying machine does have control over my life for a time.

JACOB: Cory's argument is also, I think, best described by saying that there are no more cars, there are no more airplanes, there are no more hearing aids; there are computers with four wheels, computers with wings, and computers that help you to hear. And part of this is not whether or not they are single-purpose computers; it's whether or not we can verify that they do the thing that they say that they do, and whether or not we understand how well they do it. Often people try to argue that they have the right to lock that up and to keep it a secret, and they make computers either complex or they make it legally difficult to understand them. That is actually dangerous for society because we know that people don't always act in everyone's best interests, and we also know that people make mistakes—not maliciously—and so locking these things up is very dangerous on a number of levels, not the least of which is that we are all imperfect. That's just a fact. The ability to have access to the blueprints of the systems underlying our lives is part of why free software is important, but it's also why free hardware is important. It improves our ability to freely make sustainable investments, to improve the systems we use and to determine if these systems work as expected.

But regardless of freedom, it's also why it is important to understand these systems, because when we don't understand them there's a general trend to defer to authority, to people who do understand them or are able to assert control over them, even if they do not understand the essence of the thing itself. Which is why we see so much hype about cyber war—it's because some people that seem to be in the authority about war start talking about technology as if they understand it. Such people are often talking about cyber war and not one of them, not a single one, is talking about cyber peace-building, or anything related to peace-building. They are always talking about war because that's their business and they are trying to control technological and legal processes as a means for promoting their own interests. So when we have no control over our technology such people wish to use it for their ends, for war specifically. That's a recipe for some pretty scary stuff—which is how I think we ended up with Stuxnet—and otherwise reasonable people suggest, while the US wages war, that such tactics will somehow prevent wars. That's perhaps a reasonable argument for a country that isn't actively invading other nations, but hardly credible in the context of a nation involved in multiple ongoing concurrent invasions.

THE MILITARIZATION OF CYBERSPACE

JULIAN: I see that there is now a militarization of cyberspace, in the sense of a military occupation. When you communicate over the internet, when you communicate using mobile phones, which are now meshed to the internet, your communications are being intercepted by military intelligence organizations. It's like having a tank in your bedroom. It's a soldier between you and your wife as you're SMSing. We are all living under martial law as far as our communications are concerned, we just can't see the tanks—but they are there. To that degree, the internet, which was supposed to be a civilian space, has become a militarized space. But the internet is our space, because we all use it to communicate with each other and with the members of our family. The communications at the inner core of our private lives now move over the internet. So in fact our private lives have entered into a militarized zone. It is like having a soldier under the bed. This is a militarization of civilian life.

JACOB: Right before I came here I was asked to be a coach for the Pacific Rim Collegiate Cyber Defense competition for the team of University of Washington Security and Privacy Research Laboratory. At the very last minute I was asked to be an advisor. We contributed quite a lot of time to compete in a cyber war event where SPAWAR, a civilian arm of the US Navy that includes pentesting services, who do offensive computer hacking as well as defensive computer hacking, played what is generally called the Red Team.[36] What they do is they attack everybody else that's playing and every team's job is to defend their computer systems, which have been given to them at the beginning of the event with no real foreknowledge at all. You don't know what kind of systems you'll defend and it's not even clear how the points are scored in the beginning so you just try to do your best and hope.

JULIAN: Are you sure that it's actually a game? Maybe it's not a game!

JACOB: No, you just get a bunch of computers and you have to protect them, and they break in and they take over the systems. It's like a kids' version of Capture the Flag at a real hacker conference or something like that, and it's interesting because these guys have a lot of tools, they've written software.[37]

JULIAN: What's the point of it though—from the US Navy's perspective?

JACOB: Well, in their case they are just sponsoring this because they want to build tomorrow's cyber warriors today and so, for example, I brought you a notepad from the CIA because they were recruiting. There was a guy there named Charlie—Charlie from the CIA—and he was explaining that if you want to come and join the CIA this is a great opportunity to work in the real world. And the SPAWAR people were there, and Microsoft was there recruiting. The idea was to train all of these people, all of these teams, to go on to the National Championship and to be winners and to "defend the nation," and then also to be able to go on to do offensive hacking as cyber warriors, not just cyber defenders. We scored something like 4,000 points in this game, which was the combined score of the second place, third place and fourth place teams. We were actually still higher than all of them combined.

JULIAN: Yeah, yeah, yeah.

JACOB: It wasn't thanks to me—my motivational quote was like, "Hey, it's always darkest straight before it goes pitch black," and I don't think I'm particularly good at coaching—these guys are really good. But it was interesting because the way that the whole thing was framed was in terms of war, so they would say, "Hey, we want to hear your war whoop." It's like, "I'm sorry, what?" That's what they were saying over lunch, for example, when we were taking a break from defending our systems. They framed everything in terms of attacking systems and war and cyber war and the greatness of this way of thinking. And interestingly enough, aside from the team that I was working with, I felt like there were a lot of people that were struggling, because they weren't teaching them to use the Art of War—it was more like the Sysadmin Cup, people who defend systems—and it just felt disgusting.[38] It felt really weird because there were all these people whose background is in war, and they come from the war perspective, but they're not teaching strategy, they're very focused on the rhetoric of defending these systems, or on attacking these systems, and they just had so much war in the way that they were really trying to rile people up into a sort of patriotic fervor. They weren't promoting creative thinking or some kind of framework for independent analysis; they were pushing a cog-in-the-machine-mentality of someone who follows orders for the good of the nation. I had never experienced it before. I felt sick and most of my team had a hard time stomaching it or even taking it seriously.

JULIAN: Do you think that that's standard US Navy training, and they're just now trying to apply it to another domain? Is it a top-down US cyber command decision—an international strategic decision—by the United States?

ANDY: More like the Nazis who had those youth camps where the kids were trained.

JACOB: Sie können das sagen weil du bist Deutsche. You can say that because you're German. No, it's not like that. The US Navy's involvement is just because the US government is sponsoring all this stuff. They asked me to coach because they needed someone there to do this coaching and I just agreed because I liked the guys involved, these undergrads. But really what it comes down to is that the US government is really trying to push getting people into this and they're trying to push from the perspective of nationalism. It's a very, very strange event to be at because, on the one hand, it's good to be able to know how to keep your system safe and it's good to understand the infrastructure that all of our lives rely on; but on the other hand, they weren't trying to convince people to understand it, they were trying to whip them up into a sort of fervor in order to make them happy to do this type of work.

ANDY: Unfortunately, the interest of the United States to keep systems secure is totally limited because they want systems to be vulnerable in order to take over control. The approach to controlling encryption worldwide has not been going as far as the United States originally pushed for around 1998, when the US undersecretary of commerce for international trade David Aarons went on a world tour arguing for government access to everyone's encryption passwords.[39] But encryption is still handled as a so called dual-use technology and its export in the form of end-user-products to many countries is limited by law, agreed to worldwide in the so called Wassenaar Arrangement.[40] This might sound reasonable in the context of declaring countries and their actions as "evil," but it shows the dimension of the double-standard, as telecommunication surveillance technology is so far not limited by export-controls.[41]

JULIAN: Andy, for years you've designed cryptographic telephones. What sort of mass surveillance is occurring in relation to telecommunications? Tell me what is the state of the art as far as the government intelligence/bulk-surveillance industry is concerned?

ANDY: Mass storage—meaning storing all telecommunication, all voice calls, all traffic data, any way groups consume the Short Message Service (SMS), but also internet connections, in some situations at least limited to email. If you compare the military budget to the cost of surveillance and the cost of cyber warriors, normal weapon systems cost a lot of money. Cyber warriors or mass surveillance are super-cheap compared to just one aircraft. One military aircraft costs you between…

JULIAN: Around a hundred million.

ANDY: And storage gets cheaper every year. Actually, we made some calculations in the Chaos Computer Club: you get decent voice-quality storage of all German telephone calls in a year for about 30 million euros including administrative overheads, so the pure storage is about 8 million euros.[42]

JULIAN: And there are even companies like VASTech in South Africa that are selling these systems for $10 million per year.[43] "We'll intercept all your calls, we'll store all your intercepted calls en masse." But there has been a shift in the last few years from intercepting everything going across from one country to another and picking out the particular people you want to spy on and assigning them to human beings, to now intercepting everything and storing everything permanently.

ANDY: To explain it roughly historically, in the old days someone was a target because of his diplomatic position, because of the company he worked for, because he was suspected of doing something or he was in contact with people who actually did something, and then you applied surveillance measures on him. These days it's deemed much more efficient to say, "We'll take everything and we can sort it out later." So they do have long-term storage, and the main way of describing the industry's two chapters is the "tactical" approach and the "strategic" approach. Tactical means, "Right now, in this meeting, we need to bug the place, we need to get someone in with a microphone, an array jacket, or have GSM (Global System for Mobile communications) surveillance systems, in a car, deployed, able to intercept what people are saying right away without needing to interfere with the network operator, get a police search warrant or anything like that, no legal procedure required, just do it." The strategic approach is to do it by default, just record everything, and sort it out later using analytic systems.

JULIAN: So, strategic interception is take everything that a telecommunication satellite is relaying, take everything across a fiber optic cable.

ANDY: Because you never know when someone is a suspect.

JACOB: There's a thing called the NSA AT&T case in the United States—the second case: Hepting v. AT&T. In Folsom, California, Mark Klein, a former technician for the giant telecommunications company AT&T, exposed that the NSA, the US National Security Agency, was capturing all of the data that they could get AT&T to give them. They just took it all wholesale—data as well as voice calls—so every time I picked up the phone or connected to the internet in San Francisco during the time period that Mark Klein has exposed, we know that the NSA on US soil against US citizens was getting it all.[44] I'm pretty sure they have used that intercept data in the investigations that they've been doing against people in the United States, which raises all kinds of interesting constitutional issues because they get to keep it forever.

JÉRÉMIE: We also have this example of Eagle, the system sold by the French company Amesys that was sold to Gaddafi's Libya, and on the commercial document it was written, "Nationwide interception mechanism." It's a big box that you put somewhere and you just listen to all your people's communications.[45]

JULIAN: Ten years ago this was seen to be a fantasy, this was seen to be something only paranoid people believed in, but the costs of mass interception have now decreased to the point where even a country like Libya with relatively few resources was doing it with French technology. In fact most countries are already there in terms of the actual interception. It's the efficiency of understanding and responding to what's being intercepted and stored that's going to be the next big leap. Now in many countries we have strategic interception of all traffic in and out of the country, but engaging in subsequent actions, like automatically blocking bank accounts, or deploying police, or marginalizing particular groups, or emancipating others, is still something we are on the cusp of. Siemens is selling a platform for intelligence agencies that does actually produce automated actions. So when target A is within a certain number of meters of target B according to their mobile intercept records, and target A receives an email mentioning something—a keyword—then an action is triggered. It's on the way.

FIGHTING TOTAL SURVEILLANCE WITH THE LAWS OF MAN

JÉRÉMIE: So now it's a fact that technology enables total surveillance of every communication. Then there is the other side of that coin, which is what we do with it. We could admit that for what you call tactical surveillance there are some legitimate uses—investigators investigating bad guys and networks of bad guys and so on may need, under the supervision of the judicial authority, to be able to use such tools—but the question is where to draw the line for this judicial supervision, where to draw the line for the control that the citizens can have over the use of those technologies. This is a policy issue. When we get to those policy issues you have politicians that are asked to just sign something and don't understand the underlying technology, and I think that we as citizens have a role, not only to explain how the technology functions at large, including to politicians, but also to wade in to the political debates that surround the use of those technologies. I know that in Germany there was a massive movement against generalized data retention that led to the overturn of the Data Retention law in front of the constitutional court.[46] There is a debate going on in the EU about revising the Data Retention Directive.[47]

ANDY: You are describing the theory of the democratic state which, of course, does need to filter out some bad guys here and there and listen to their phone calls on the basis of a court decision with overview to make sure it is done in the proper way. The trouble with that is that the authorities need to act in compliance with the law. If they don't do that then what are they good for? Especially with this strategic approach, democratic states within Europe are massively buying machines that allow them to act exactly outside the law in regard to interception because they don't need a court decision, they can just switch it on and do it, and this technology can't be controlled.

JULIAN: But are there two approaches to dealing with mass state surveillance: the laws of physics; and the laws of man? One is to use the laws of physics by actually building devices that prevent interception. The other is to enact democratic controls through the law to make sure people must have warrants and so on and to try to gain some regulatory accountability. But strategic interception cannot be a part of that, cannot be meaningfully constrained by regulation. Strategic interception is about intercepting *everyone* regardless of whether they are innocent or guilty. We must remember that it is the core of the Establishment carrying such surveillance. There will always be a lack of political will to expose state spying. And the technology is inherently so complex, and its use in practice so secret that there cannot be meaningful democratic oversight.

ANDY: Or you spy on your own parliament.

JULIAN: But those are excuses—the mafia and foreign intelligence—they are excuses that people will accept to erect such a system.

JACOB: The Four Horsemen of the Info-pocalypse: child pornography, terrorism, money laundering, and The War on Some Drugs.

JULIAN: Once you have erected this surveillance, given that it is complex, given that it is designed to operate in secret, isn't it true that it cannot be regulated with policy? I think that except for very small nations like Iceland, unless there are revolutionary conditions it is simply not possible to control mass interception with legislation and policy. It is just not going to happen. It is too cheap and too easy to get around political accountability and to actually perform interception. The Swedes got through an interception bill in 2008, known as the FRA-lagen, which meant the Swedish signals intelligence agency the FRA could legally intercept all communication travelling through the country in bulk, and ship it off to the United States, with some caveats.[48] Now how can you enforce those caveats once you've set up the interception system and the organization doing it is a secret spy agency? It's impossible. And in fact cases have come out showing that the FRA had on a variety of occasions broken the law previously. Many countries simply do it off-law with no legislative cover at all. So we're sort of lucky if, like in the Swedish example, they decided that for their own protection from prosecution they want to go legal by changing the law. And that's the case for most countries—there is bulk interception occurring, and when there is a legislative proposal it is to protect the ass of those who are doing it.

This technology is very complex; for example in the debate in Australia and the UK about proposed legislation to intercept all metadata, most people do not understand the value of metadata or even the word itself.[49] Intercepting all metadata means you have to build a system that physically intercepts all data and then throws everything but the metadata away. But such a system cannot be trusted. There's no way to determine whether it is in fact intercepting and storing all data without having highly skilled engineers with authorization to go in and check out precisely what is going on, and there's no political will to grant access. The problem is getting worse because complexity and secrecy are a toxic mix. Hidden by complexity. Hidden by secrecy. Unaccountability is built-in. It is a feature. It is dangerous by design.

JÉRÉMIE: I'm not saying that the policy approach can work. I'm saying that this is the theory of how a democratic system would function, and indeed, even within this theory you have the secret services that are allowed to go beyond what is the rule for standard police forces and investigators. So even if we frame the behavior of the standard investigators properly, there would be other people who would be able to use those technologies. But there is a real question of whether or not we should regulate the fact of just buying and owning those technologies as opposed to regulating the use of them.

JULIAN: This is the bulk interception kits that can intercept half a country or a city.

JÉRÉMIE: Yes. Like a nuclear weapon: you cannot sell a nuclear weapon easily, and some countries may want to build one but have problems. When we talk about weapons systems it's the technology that is regulated and not the use that is made of it. I think the debate might be about whether or not these technologies should be considered as war.

JACOB: It depends. When it is weapons—and there is no question that surveillance equipment is a weapon in places like Syria or Libya—they specifically use it to target people politically. The French company, Amesys, targeted people in the United Kingdom using French equipment that would be illegal to run in France, and they sold it knowingly.[50]

ANDY: And they'd never do that, right?

JACOB: Well, Amesys were caught with their own internal documents in The Spy Files.[51] If we're going to talk about it in terms of weapons, we have to remember it is not like selling a country a truck. It's like selling a country a truck, a mechanic and a team that goes in the truck that selectively targets people and then shoots them.

JULIAN: It's like selling it a whole army of trucks.

ANDY: It's interesting that cryptography is regulated. There's the Wassenaar Arrangement, which applies internationally, meaning you cannot export encryption technology, which helps to protect against surveillance technology, to those countries declared evil or, for whatever reason, problematic. But if you are dealing surveillance equipment you *can* sell that internationally. There are no export restrictions on that. The reason, I would say, is simply because even the democratically-run governments have a self-interest, which is to control. And even if you're dealing with evil countries and you bring them surveillance equipment to do evil things you will benefit, because you will learn what they are listening to, what are they afraid of, who are the most important people in the country opposing the government, organizing political events and so on. So you will be able to predict future happenings, to sponsor actions and so on. Here we are in the very dirty game of what is happening between countries, and that's the reality of why surveillance systems are not regulated.

JULIAN: I want to explore this analogy of mass surveillance being a weapon of mass destruction. It was a fact of physics that it was possible to make an atomic bomb, and when an atomic bomb was made then geo-politics changed, and life for many people changed—in different ways, some positive perhaps, and others on the brink of total apocalypse. A regulatory movement applied controls and so far those controls have, with the exception of Japan, saved us from nuclear war. But it's easy to tell when such weapons are used and when they are not.

With the increase in the sophistication and the reduction of the cost of bulk surveillance that has happened over the past ten years, we're now at a stage where the human population is doubling every twenty-five years or so—but the capacity of surveillance is doubling every eighteen months. The surveillance curve is dominating the population curve. There is no direct escape. We're now at the stage where just $10 million can buy you a unit to permanently store the mass intercepts of a medium sized country. So I wonder if we need an equivalent response. This really is a big threat to democracy and to freedom all around the world that needs a response, like the threat of atomic war needed a mass response, to try and control it, while we still can.

ANDY: I was seeing in Libya how the democratic movement ran into the surveillance stations, they took records, they provided evidence that Western companies supported the Gaddafi regime in suppressing political actions, and then the new government took over exactly these facilities which are now operating in full service again.[52] So while I do agree that it would be a good idea to control this technology, I am a bit skeptical about the interests of citizens against the interests of people in power. I wouldn't even call it governments necessarily, because whoever has the ability to listen to all the phone calls has the ability to do things. This is about stock rates also—economically, you can benefit a lot if you know what's going on.

JULIAN: Where countries have legislation as to what the targets of their major electronic spy agencies are supposed to be—agencies like the NSA in the United States, GCHQ (Government Communications Headquarters) in the United Kingdom, the DSD (Defense Signals Directorate) in Australia—they have changed that legislation to include economic intelligence. For example, say Australia and the US are vying for a wheat deal, they snoop on all the people who are involved in the deal. This has been around for a long time now, at least ten years in public—but it is granted because people are doing it anyway. It started with arms deals, where you have companies like

Lockheed Martin, Raytheon, and Northrup doing arms deals, and also being involved in building mass interception systems because these groups are close at a patronage level. They got favors from their friends and covered arms deal intercepts under national security criteria. But now it applies to anything that could economically benefit a country, which is almost everything.

JACOB: A good analogy that some people in the Chaos Communication Congress brought up in December 2011 was the concept of treating surveillance technology, especially tactical surveillance technology but also strategic surveillance technology, like land-mines.[53] I think that's a very powerful thing. Just because it's possible doesn't mean that it's inevitable that we will go down this path, and it doesn't mean that we have to get all the way to the point of every person being monitored.

There are some economic incentives that are against us though. For example, someone explained to me that the way that the Norwegian telephone system used to work is such that it would essentially run a meter which, depending on how far away your call, would run faster or slower. But it was not legal for the Norwegian telephone company to store or to keep a ledger of the actual meta-data about the call you made, such as the number you dialed, specifically because of privacy concerns surrounding the Second World War. So it is possible to build that same technology in a way that is privacy-friendly but still allows for a market-based approach, which still allows for economic contributions. However we cannot win, for example, with GSM (mobile) technologies. At the moment the way that these systems are set up, not just in terms of billing but in terms of the architecture, means they have no location privacy, they have no content privacy.

JULIAN: A mobile phone is a tracking device that also makes calls.

JACOB: Exactly. For example, if we're talking about everybody in the Third World being spied on, realistically what does that mean? It means their telephone systems, which are their link to the rest of the world, are spy devices when someone chooses to use the data collected in that way.

ANDY: I saw African countries are getting a whole internet infra-structure, including fiber optic cable and backbone switches, as a gift from the Chinese.

JACOB: As a ZTE gift or something like that?[54]

ANDY: Yes, and of course the Chinese have an interest in the data, so they don't need to be paid back in money, they take it in data, the new currency.

PRIVATE SECTOR SPYING

JÉRÉMIE: State-sponsored surveillance is indeed a major issue which challenges the very structure of all democracies and the way they function, but there is also private surveillance and potentially private mass collection of data. Just look at Google. If you're a standard Google user Google knows who you're communicating with, who you know, what you're researching, potentially your sexual orientation, and your religious and philosophical beliefs.

ANDY: It knows more about you than you know yourself.

JÉRÉMIE: More than your mother and maybe more than yourself. Google knows when you're online and when you're not.

ANDY: Do you know what you looked for two years, three days and four hours ago? You don't know; Google knows.

JÉRÉMIE: Actually, I try not to use Google anymore for these very reasons.

JACOB: It's like the Kill Your Television of the 21st century.[55] Effective protest except the network effect prevents your protest from working.[56] Kill your television, man.

JÉRÉMIE: Well it's not a protest, it is more my personal way of seeing things.

ANDY: I watched these beautiful movies of people throwing their televisions out of three-storey houses.

JÉRÉMIE: It's not only the state-sponsored surveillance, it's the question of privacy, the way data is being handled by third parties and the knowledge that people have of what is being done with the data. I don't use Facebook so I don't know much about it. But now with Facebook you see the behavior of users who are very happy to hand out any kind of personal data, and can you blame people for not knowing where the limit is between privacy and publicity? A few years ago, before digital technologies, people who had a public life were either in show-business, politics or journalism, and now everybody has the potential for public life by clicking a publish button. "Publish" means make something public, it means handing out access to this data to the rest of the world—and, of course, when you see teenagers sending pictures of themselves drunk or whatever, they may not have this vision that it means the whole of the rest of the world, potentially for a very, very long period of time. Facebook makes its business by blurring this line between privacy, friends, and publicity. And it is even storing the data when you think that it is only meant for your friends and the people you love. So whatever the degree of publicity that you intend your data to be under, when you click publish on Facebook you give it to Facebook first, and then they give access to some other Facebook users after.

JULIAN: Even this line between government and corporation is blurred. If you look at the expansion in the military contractor sector in the West over the past ten years, the NSA, which was the biggest spy agency in the world, had ten primary contractors on its books that it worked with. Two years ago it had over 1,000. So there is a smearing out of the border between what is government and what is the private sector.

JÉRÉMIE: And it can be argued that the US spying agencies have access to all of Google's stored data.

JULIAN: But they do.

JÉRÉMIE: And all of Facebook's data, so in a way Facebook and Google may be extensions of these agencies.

JULIAN: Do you have a Google subpoena Jake? Was a subpoena sent to Google to hand over information related to your Google account? WikiLeaks got subpoenas to our California domain name registrar dynadot, which is where the wikileaks.org registration is made. They were subpoenas from the secret ongoing Grand Jury investigation into WikiLeaks, asking for financial records, login records, et cetera, which it gave them.[57]

JACOB: The *Wall Street Journal* reported that Twitter and Google and Sonic.net, three services that I use or have used in the past, each received a 2703(d) notice, which is this unusual form of secret subpoena.[58]

JULIAN: Under the PATRIOT Act?

JACOB: No. This is the Stored Communications Act, essentially. The *Wall Street Journal* is saying that each of these services claims that the government wanted the metadata, and the government asserted it has the right to do this without a warrant. There's an ongoing legal case about the government's right to keep its tactics secret, not only from the public, but from court records. I read the *Wall Street Journal* and found out like everyone else.

JULIAN: So Google sucked up to the US government in its Grand Jury investigation into WikiLeaks when the government subpoenaed your records—not a conventional subpoena, but this special sort of intelligence subpoena. But the news came out earlier in 2011 that Twitter had been served a number of subpoenas, from the same Grand Jury, but Twitter fought to be able to notify the people whose accounts were subpoenaed—for the gag order to be lifted. I don't have a Twitter account, so I didn't get one, but my name and Bradley Manning's name were on all the subpoenas as the information that was being searched for. Jake, you had a Twitter account so Twitter received a subpoena in relation to you. Google also received a subpoena, but didn't fight to make it public.[59]

JACOB: Allegedly. That's what I read in the *Wall Street Journal*. I might not be even allowed to reference it except for in connection to the *Wall Street Journal*.

JULIAN: Is it because these orders also have a gag component? That has been found to be unconstitutional, hasn't it?

JACOB: Maybe not. For the Twitter case it is public that we lost the motion for a stay where we said that disclosing this data to the government would do irreparable harm as they can never forget this data once they receive it. They said, "Yeah well, your stay is denied, Twitter must disclose this data." We're in the process of appeal, specifically about the secrecy of docketing—and I can't talk about that—but as it stands right now, the court said that on the internet you have no expectation of privacy when you willingly reveal information to a third party, and, by the way, everyone on the internet is a third party.

JULIAN: Even if the organization like Facebook or Twitter says that it will keep the information private.

JACOB: For sure. And this is the blurring of the state and corporation. This is actually probably the most important thing to consider here, that the NSA and Google have a partnership in cyber-security for US national defense reasons.

ANDY: Whatever cyber-security means in this context. That's a wide term.

JACOB: They are trying to exempt everything from the Freedom of Information Act and to keep it secret. Then the US government also asserts it has the right to send an administrative subpoena, which has a lower bar than a search warrant, where the third party is gagged from telling you about it, and you have no right to fight because it is the third party that is directly involved, and the third party has no constitutional grounds to protect your data either.

JULIAN: The third party being Twitter or Facebook or your ISP.

JACOB: Or anyone. They said it was a one-to-one map with banking privacy and with dialing a telephone. You willingly disclose the number to the phone company by using it. You knew that, right? By using the telephone you obviously are saying, "I have no expectation of privacy," when typing those numbers. There is even less explicit connection to the machine. People don't understand how the internet works—they don't understand telephone networks either—but courts have consistently ruled that this is the case, and in our Twitter case so far, which unfortunately I can't really talk about because I don't actually live in a free country, they assert essentially the same thing.[60]

It's absolute madness to imagine that we give up all of our personal data to these companies, and then the companies have essentially become privatized secret police. And—in the case of Facebook—we even have democratized surveillance. Instead of paying people off the way the Stasi did in East Germany, we reward them as a culture—they get laid now. They report on their friends and then, "Hey, so and so got engaged;" "Oh, so and so broke up;" "Oh, I know who to call now."

ANDY: There were people who were able to pressure Facebook to hand out all the data stored about them under European Data Protection law, and the smallest amount of data was 350 MB, the biggest one was around 800 MB.[61] The interesting thing is the database structure of Facebook has been disclosed with this act. Every time you log in the IP number and everything gets stored, every click you make, every time, also the amount of times you stay on a page so they can assume you like it, you don't like it and so on. But this disclosed that the key identifier of the database structure was the word "target." They don't call these people "subscribers" or "users" or whatever, they call them "targets," to which you could say, "Ok, that's a marketing term."

JULIAN: But it was internally private.

ANDY: Yes, but in a military sense it could also be target, or it could be in an intelligence sense target. So it is just is a matter of the circumstances in which the data is being used.

JULIAN: OK. That's what's so scary about it.

ANDY: I think that is very helpful. We used to say with Facebook that the user is not actually the customer. The Facebook user is actually the product, and the real customer is the advertising companies. That's the least paranoid, most harmless explanation of what's going on there.

But the problem is you can hardly blame a company for complying with the laws of the country. It's called normal, and it's called criminal if companies don't comply with the laws of the country.

So it's a little bit of a hard thing to say, "Hey, they're complying with the law." What kind of accusation is that?

JACOB: No, there is something I have to dispute about that. If you build a system that logs everything about a person and you know that you live in a country with laws that will force the government to give that up, then maybe you shouldn't build that kind of system. And this is the difference between a privacy-by-policy and a privacy-by-design approach to creating secure systems. When you're trying to target people and you know that you live in a country that explicitly targets people, then if Facebook puts its servers in Gaddafi's Libya or puts them in Assad's Syria that would be absolutely negligent. And yet none of the National Security Letters that went out, I think last year or two years ago, were for terrorism. Like, 250,000 of them were used for everything else, but not terrorism.[62] So knowing that's reality, these companies have some serious ethical liability that stems from the fact that they're building these systems and they've made the economic choice to basically sell their users out. And this isn't even a technical thing. This isn't about technology at all, it's about economics. They have decided that it is more important to collaborate with the state and to sell out their users and to violate their privacy and to be a part of the system of control—to be paid back for being a part of the surveillance culture, to be part of the culture of control—than to be resistant to it, and so they become a part of it. They're complicit and liable.

ANDY: Ethical liability is not exactly a major selling point right now, huh?

FIGHTING TOTAL SURVEILLANCE WITH THE LAWS OF PHYSICS

JÉRÉMIE: A question that may arise at this stage is what is the solution, either for an individual user or for society as a whole? There are technical solutions—decentralized services, everybody hosting their own data, encrypted data, everybody trusting providers close to them that help them with encrypted data services, and so on. And there are the policy options that we have discussed. I'm not sure that at this stage in time that we can answer the question of whether one of the two approaches is the best. I think we have to develop the two approaches in parallel. We need to have free software that everybody can understand, everybody can modify, and everybody can scrutinize in order to be sure of what it is doing. I think free software is one of the bases for a free online society, in order to have the potential to always control the machine and not let the machine control you. We need to have strong cryptography to be sure that when you want your data to be read only by yourself, nobody else can read it. We need communication tools like Tor, or like the Cryptophone, to be able to communicate only with the people you want to communicate with. But the power of the state and the power of some companies may always exceed the power of the geeks we are, and our ability to build and spread those technologies. We may also need, while we are building those technologies, laws and tools that will be in the hands of citizens, to be able to control what is being done with technology—if not always in real time—and to be able to sanction those that use technology in an unethical way and in a way that violates citizens' privacy.

JULIAN: I want to look at what I see as a difference between a US cypherpunk perspective and the European perspective. The US Second Amendment is the right to bear arms. Just recently I was watching some footage that a friend shot in the US on the right to bear arms, and above a firearms store was a sign saying, "Democracy, Locked and Loaded." That's the way that you ensure that you don't have totalitarian regimes—people are armed and if they are pissed off enough then they simply take their arms and they retake control by force. Whether that argument is still valid now is actually an interesting question because of the difference in the types of arms that has occurred over the past thirty years. We can look back to this declaration that code-making—providing secret cryptographic codes that the government couldn't spy on—was in fact a munition. We fought this big war in the 1990s to try and make cryptography available to everyone, which we largely won.[63]

JACOB: In the West.

JULIAN: In the West we largely won and it is in every browser, although perhaps it is now being back-doored and subverted in different kinds of ways.[64] The notion is that you cannot trust a government to implement the policies that it says it is implementing, and so we must provide the underlying tools, cryptographic tools that we control, as a sort of use of force, in that if the ciphers are good no matter how hard it tries a government cannot break into your communications directly.

JACOB: The force of nearly all modern authority is derived from violence or the threat of violence. One must acknowledge with cryptography no amount of violence will ever solve a math problem.

JULIAN: Exactly.

JACOB: This is the important key. It doesn't mean you can't be tortured, it doesn't mean that they can't try to bug your house or subvert it in some way, but it means that if they find an encrypted message it doesn't matter if they have the force of the authority behind everything that they do, they cannot solve that math problem. This, though, is the thing that is totally non-obvious to people that are non-technical, and it has to be driven home. If we could solve all of those math problems, it would be a different story and, of course, the government would be able to solve those math problems if anyone could.

JULIAN: But it just happens to be a fact about reality, such as that you can build atomic bombs, that there are math problems that you can create that even the strongest state cannot break. I think that was tremendously appealing to Californian libertarians and others who believed in this sort of "democracy locked and loaded" idea, because here was a very intellectual way of doing it—of a couple of individuals with cryptography standing up to the full might of the strongest power in the world.

So there is a property of the universe that is on the side of privacy, because some encryption algorithms are impossible for any government to break, ever. There are others that we know are extremely hard for even the NSA to break. We know that because they recommend those algorithms be used by US military contractors for the protection of top secret US military communications, and if there was some kind of back-door in them soon enough the Russians or the Chinese would find it, with severe consequences for whoever made the decision to recommend an insecure cipher. So the ciphers are fairly good now, we're pretty confident in them. Unfortunately you can't be confident at all in the machine that you're running them on, so that's a problem. But that doesn't lead to bulk interception; it leads to the targeting of particular people's computers. Unless you're a security expert it's very hard to actually secure a computer. But cryptography can solve the bulk interception problem, and it's the bulk interception problem which is a threat to global civilization. Individual targeting is not the threat.

Nevertheless, I have a view that we are dealing with really tremendously big economic and political forces, as Jérémie said, and the likely outcome is that the natural efficiencies of surveillance technologies compared to the number of human beings will mean that slowly we will end up in a global totalitarian surveillance society—by totalitarian I mean a total surveillance—and that perhaps there will just be the last free living people, those who understand how to use this cryptography to defend against this complete, total surveillance, and some people who are completely off-grid, neo-Luddites that have gone into the cave, or traditional tribes-people who have none of the efficiencies of a modern economy and so their ability to act is very small. Of course anyone can stay off the internet, but then it's hard for them to have any influence. They select themselves out of being influential by doing that. It's the same with mobile phones; you can choose not to have a mobile phone but you reduce your influence. It's not a way forward.

JÉRÉMIE: If you look at it from a market perspective, I'm convinced that there is a market in privacy that has been mostly left unexplored, so maybe there will be an economic drive for companies to develop tools that will give users the individual ability to control their data and communication. Maybe this is one way that we can solve that problem. I'm not sure it can work alone, but this may happen and we may not know it yet.

JULIAN: Cryptography is going to be everywhere. It is being deployed by major organizations everywhere, edging towards networked city states. If you think about communication paths on the internet—fast transnational money flows, transnational organizations, inter-connections between sub-parts of organizations—all those communication flows go over untrusted communications channels. It is like an organism with no skin. You have organizations and states blurring into each other—each network of world influence competing for advantage—and their communications flows are exposed to opportunists, state competitors and so on. So new networks are being built up on top of the internet, virtual private networks, and their privacy comes from cryptography. That is an industrial power base that is stopping cryptography from being banned.

If you look at the Blackberry phone for example, it has a built-in encryption system for use within the Blackberry network. Research In Motion, the Canadian company that runs it, can decrypt the traffic of regular users and it has data centers in Canada and the UK, at least, and so the Anglo-American intelligence sharing alliance can get at the world's Blackberry to Blackberry communications. But big companies are using it in more secure ways. Western governments were fine with this until it spread beyond corporations and to individuals, and then we saw exactly the same hostile political reactions as we saw in Mubarak's Egypt.[65]

I think that the only effective defense against the coming surveillance dystopia is one where you take steps yourself to safeguard your privacy, because there's no incentive for self-restraint by the people that have the capacity to intercept everything. A historical analogy could be how people learned that they should wash their hands. That required the germ theory of disease to be established and then popularized, and for paranoia to be instilled about the spread of disease via invisible stuff on your hands that you can't see, just as you can't see mass interception. Once there was enough understanding, soap manufacturers produced products that people consumed to relieve their fear. It's necessary to install fear in to people so they understand the problem before they will create enough demand to solve the problem.

There is a problem on the opposite side of the equation as well, which is that programs that claim to be secure, that claim to have cryptography in them, are often frauds, because cryptography is complex, and the fraud can be hidden in complexity.[66]

So people will have to think about it. The only question is in which one of the two ways will they think about it? They will either think, "I need to be careful about what I say, I need to conform," the whole time, in every interaction. Or they will think "I need to master little components of this technology and install things that protect me so I'm able to express my thoughts freely and communicate freely with my friends and people I care about." If people don't take that second step then we'll have a universal political correctness, because even when people are communicating with their closest friends they will be self-censors and will remove themselves as political actors from the world.

THE INTERNET AND POLITICS

JÉRÉMIE: It is interesting to see the power of the hackers—"hackers" in the primary sense of the term, not a criminal. A hacker is a technology enthusiast, somebody who likes to understand how technology works, not to be trapped into technology but to make it work better. I suppose that when you were five or seven you had a screwdriver and tried to open devices to understand what it was like inside. This is what being a hacker is, and hackers built the internet for many reasons, including because it was fun, and they have developed it and have given the internet to everybody else. Companies like Google and Facebook saw the opportunity to then build business models based on capturing users' personal data. But still we see a form of power in the hands of hackers. My primary interest these days is that we see these hackers gaining power, even in the political arenas. In the US there has been this SOPA (Stop Online Piracy Act) and PIPA (Protect IP Act) legislation—violent copyright legislation that basically gives Hollywood the power to order any internet company to restrict access and to censor the internet.[67]

JULIAN: And banking blockades like the one WikiLeaks is suffering from.[68]

JÉRÉMIE: Exactly. What happened to WikiLeaks from the banking companies was becoming the standard method to fight the evil copyright pirates that killed Hollywood and so on. And we witnessed this tremendous uproar from civil society on the internet—and not only in the US, it couldn't have worked if it was only US citizens who rose up against SOPA and PIPA. It was people all around the world that participated, and hackers were at the core of it and were providing tools to the others to help participate in the public debate.

JULIAN: To help build the campaign.

JÉRÉMIE: Was it on Tumblr or some site like this where the home page lets you enter your phone number and you'll be called back and put in touch with the Congress? And you would just start talking with somebody and say, "Yeah, this is bullshit."

JACOB: The internet was used in defense of itself.

JÉRÉMIE: I think we hackers have a responsibility towards the tools we build and hand out to the rest of the world, and we may be witnessing the beginning of how efficiently this responsibility can be put into action when we use it collectively. Today in the EU there is the ACTA debate—ACTA (the Anti-Counterfeiting Trade Agreement) is a multinational treaty that is the blueprint for SOPA and PIPA.[69] I just came back from the European Parliament where we as individuals, beardy smelly individuals, were dictating to one parliamentary committee. We were showing them articles in the rules of procedure in the European Parliament that apparently they were looking at for the first time and told them how to behave, and there was this vote that we won by 21 to 5 which marginalized the British Rapporteur in a small corner. This is a very small part of a small procedural point on the way towards defeating ACTA, this monstrous global agreement that has been designed behind our backs to circumvent democracy itself. But we may as citizens be able to kill that monster—easily, with the internet tools, the mailing lists, the wikis, the IRC chat rooms, et cetera—and I think that we may be witnessing the coming of age, the teenage years of the internet and the way that it can be used by society at large to try to make things change. I think it is of tremendous importance that we hackers are here with our technical knowledge to guide people and to tell them, "You should use this technology that enables control over your privacy rather than Facebook or Google," and that the two articulate together quite well—or may articulate together quite well. This is a small bit of optimism.

JULIAN: Jake, on this political radicalization of internet youth, over the past two years especially you've been all over the world talking about Tor, talking to people who want anonymity, who want privacy in relation to their own government, and you must have seen this phenomenon in many different countries. Is it something significant?

JACOB: Sure. I think it is absolutely significant. The canonical example that I think of immediately is going to Tunisia. I went to Tunisia after Ben Ali's regime fell and we talked about Tor in a computer science class, which includes some very technical people at the university, and someone raised their hand and said, "But what about the bad people?" And she rattled off the Four Horsemen of the Info-pocalypse—money laundering, drugs, terrorism and child pornography. "What about the bad people?" Those four things are always brought out and the specter of them is used to shoot down privacy-preserving technologies, because clearly we have to defeat those four groups. So I asked the class: "Who here has ever seen the Ammar 404 page?" which is the censorship page deployed by the Ben Ali regime before and during the revolution in order to stop access. Every single person in the room, except the person that asked that question, but including the professor in the class, raised their hand. And I looked at the girl who asked this question and I said, "Look at all the people around you. That's all of your classmates. Do you really believe that it was worth oppressing every person in this room in order to fight against those things?" And she said, "Actually, I'm raising my hand too".

It was a little more drawn out than that but essentially people who have it contextualized for them realize what the real deal is. That changes things dramatically. And this happens all over the world, all the time—but it usually happens later, that is people see in hindsight that they could have used the technology, they see in hindsight that, "Oh yeah, it turns out it's not just bad people because, in fact, I am the bad person if I speak my mind about something and a person in power doesn't like what I have to say about it." And you see that there's an awakening.

But it is wrong to say that it just happened in the last couple of years. I'm sorry to do this to you Julian, but you are part of the radicalization of my generation. I'm like a third-generation cypherpunk if I were to count it that way. The work that you and Ralf Weinmann did on the rubberhose file system was part of what inspired me to work on cryptosystems. The crypto file system I designed, called

M.A.I.D., was in response to things like the regulatory investigative powers in the United Kingdom, where basically the state has decided negative regulation is the solution to cryptography, where they can take your password.[70] Of course, in Julian's case when they created this it was because oppressive regimes would torture people for a passphrase so you had to be able to give up different passphrases in order to comply with their torture. My crypto file system, M.A.I.D., was designed for a legal system where the accused has the right to remain silent but can prove, if compelled, that they are telling the truth without violating confidentiality. I had realized when I saw Julian's work that you could use technology to empower everyday people to change the world. Going far, far back to the old Cypherpunk mailing list with Tim May, one of the founding members of it, and reading Julian's old posts on the Cypherpunk list, that's what started a whole generation of people to really become more radicalized, because people realized that they weren't atomized anymore, that they could take some time to write some software which could empower millions of people.[71]

There are just some unintended consequences with how that played out, because the people that created Google didn't start out to create Google, to create the greatest surveillance machine that ever existed. But in effect that is what has been created, and as soon as people start to realize it they'll start sending in those National Security Letters, right?

JÉRÉMIE: I think there are three crucial points in what you just said.

JACOB: Just three?

JÉRÉMIE: Among others.

ANDY: Ok, let me add number four maybe, yeah?

JACOB: You don't even know what they are yet.

JÉRÉMIE: I see three points that are intertwined. I'm not saying they should be taken separately, but one of them is authoritarian regimes and the powers that authoritarian regimes have in an era of digital technologies. In the case of the Ben Ali regime—it is obvious in so many regimes today—you can decide what people can learn about, or who they can communicate with. This is of tremendous power and this should be opposed, and the internet—a free internet—is a tool for opposing that. Another point is building tools and better technology, technology that can try to route around such problems as censorship, but basically building tools that are part of that infrastructure that helps us topple dictators. And yet another issue is the political storytelling you evoked with the Four Horsemen of the Info-pocalypse, the pre-texts that are used every day by politicians through the media—"Are we all going to die of terrorism? Therefore we need a Patriot Act;" "Child pornographers are everywhere;" "There are pedo-Nazis all over the internet, therefore we need censorship."

JACOB: Pedo-Nazis?

JÉRÉMIE: Pedo-Nazis, yeah—pedo-nazi.com is reserved already. "Artists are going to die and there won't be cinema anymore, there-fore we have to give Hollywood the power to censor the internet," and so on. I think here again the internet is a tool, an antidote to the political storytelling. The political storytelling relies on emotionality and a media time-frame that is of extremely short span—information appears and disappears twenty-four hours afterwards and is replaced by new information. With the internet, I get the feeling that we're building what I call internet time. As the great internet never forgets, we can build dossiers over years, day after day, and we can elaborate, we can analyze. This is what we've been doing for the last three years with ACTA. Once again, WikiLeaks has been an inspiration to us because the first version of ACTA that got leaked was leaked to WikiLeaks in 2008.[72]

JULIAN: Yes, we picked it up.

JÉRÉMIE: And we leaked two versions ourselves. There are five versions of the text over three years that we could take and paragraph by paragraph, line by line, say this is doing that, this is the industry asking for this, and involve legal experts and technology experts and build a version of political storytelling that was different from the official, "Oh, we need ACTA to save culture and save children from fake medications," and such. And so we built our own political line with internet time, with precise analysis, with hard work, with connecting people together to participate in that.

JULIAN: That's true, and I think that view of ACTA has won the public.

JÉRÉMIE: So far, so good.

JULIAN: That I think will be the historical view, but behind the scenes this so-called Anti-Counterfeiting Trade Agreement, which was originated by the US copyright industry, has actually been used in a whole lot of bilateral treaties to try and create a new international regime about what is legal and what is not legal as far as publishing is concerned, and what mechanisms there are to stop people from publishing various things. It standardizes a harsher version of the US DMCA system (the Digital Millennium Copyright Act), under which if you send someone a letter demanding they take something down from the internet, they have to take it down, and there is some sort of two week process where they can make counter-arguments and so on but because it is expensive for any ISP publisher to deal with the counter-argument they just take it down immediately, and they allow the author or the uploader to try and fight it out themselves. The effect of it has been quite severe in the US, in removing a whole bunch of content. Scientology abused it to remove literally thousands of videos from YouTube.[73]

So let's assume that ACTA has been knocked out in the European Parliament, actually successfully, at least this iteration. But the main developments of ACTA seem to be occurring anyway—we've had the democratic debate, ACTA has been demonized in the public sphere, we've won the narrative, but behind the scenes secret bilateral treaties have been set up which are achieving the same result, it has just subverted the democratic process. For example WikiLeaks got hold of and released the new EU-India free trade agreement, and incorporated in that are large chunks of ACTA.[74] That has been happening to a number of other agreements and legislation. The ACTA head might well get cut off but the body will split into a few bits and they will all worm their way into things, into the international order in the form of all these bilateral treaties. So you can have your democratic victories that take place in public, on the surface, but underneath things are still done anyway. Which is to show that I don't think that policy or legislative reform is the way; although you can't give the opponent a free kick either, because then they just accelerate. So it is important to check them in various ways, as ACTA is being checked. It slows them down. But even a win in parliament in relation to legislation doesn't stop this below the surface activity.

JACOB: One thing that I think really has to be pointed out is that Roger Dingledine, one of the creators of Tor, who I would say is sort of my mentor and has really given me a lot to think about with regard to censorship circumvention and anonymity online, talks about how, for example, firewalls are not just technically successful—and it is important to understand the technology behind them if you wish to build technology to resist them—but they are socially successful. People who are fighting against ACTA are using technology and the technology enables them to resist, but it is in fact the agency of everyday people that it's important to understand here, and technobabble is not the thing that is important. What matters is people actually getting involved in that narrative and changing it while they still have the power to do so, and the human aspect of that is, in fact, the most important part. WikiLeaks has released documents that enable that, and the information-sharing is important, but it is also the people who take that important information and actually move it who matter. Because there is at least the argument that many of us might live in a democracy, that we are free, that it is supposed to be that we are governed through consent. And so if everyone understands what is going on and we find it is not something we consent to, then it is very difficult to keep going and just pass those as laws and do it without the consent of those that are governed.

JÉRÉMIE: It's about increasing the political costs of taking those bad decisions for the ones who take them, and we can do that collectively with a free internet as long as we have it between our hands.

JACOB: But you could do it without an internet also, because we have—historically—had free societies pre-internet, it was just economically more expensive, it was more difficult in some ways, and this is actually why the peer-to-peer movement is so important.[75]

ANDY: Point number four is, I think, the architectural dimension of decentralized systems is a core thing that also needs to be put in the hands of the people, because now we have this centralized cloud computing.[76]

JULIAN: We have Facebook completely centralized. Twitter completely centralized. Google completely centralized. All in the United States; all controllable by whoever controls coercive force. Just like the censorship that started after WikiLeaks released Cablegate, when Amazon dropped our site from its servers.[77]

ANDY: And we have cloud computing providing an economic incentive for companies to have a cheaper way of processing their data in so-called international data centers run by US corporations, which means bringing the data into US jurisdictions, just like the payment companies and so on.

JULIAN: There is a tendency within the shift to cloud computing that is quite worrying. There are enormous clusters of servers all in one location, because it is more efficient to standardize control of the environment, to standardize the payment system. It is a competitive technique because piling up servers in the one location is cheaper than spreading them out. Most of the communication that occurs on the internet, except for streaming movies, is between server and server, so if you put the servers closer together it is cheaper. We end up with these big hives of communicating servers. It makes sense for Google, for example, to put its servers near the big content providers, or the other way around, because the pages are indexed by Google to be searchable. So there are huge buildings in the US that are just completely filled with servers from many different companies. That's where the NSA places some of its mass interception collection points. The internet could exist without this centralization, it's not that the technology is impossible, it's just that it is simply more efficient to have it centralized. In economic competition, the centralized version wins out.

ANDY: While the architectural point of view is very important to understand—centralized infrastructures make central control and abuse of power very easy—this is also like killing the small supermarket next door with a centralized retail concept.

JULIAN: And going to a big, big multinational like Safeway.

ANDY: Yes, the same way that it happened with shopping. It's very important to keep up a decentralized infrastructure approach. When I was part of ICANN, the Internet Corporation for Assigned Names and Numbers, which makes and regulates the domain names on the internet, I learned something from Vince Cerf, who invented at least part of the TCP/IP protocol, the fundamental communication protocol of the internet. He always used to say, "You know, one good thing about governments is they're never singular, they're always in plural." So even among governments, there are those that want to have their own decentralized range of power, and even within governments there are different factions fighting with each other. That is finally what is going to save us from Big Brother, because there are going to be too many who want to be Big Brother and they will have fights amongst each other.

JULIAN: I don't think so, Andy. I think once upon a time we had national elites that were competitive with each other, and now they're linking together and they're lifting off their respective populations.

ANDY: They are linking together, you are right in that respect—and I'm not so sure it's really going to save our ass—but there is the chance of actually keeping our own identity. We have to stick to our own infrastructure, that's the important thing to learn here—that if we want to oppose the surveillance state, the one Big Brother, we have to study what that is, whether it is indeed a linking of central states that say, "Hey, if we combine we can gain even more." And we need to know what our role is here—our role is to keep decentralized, have our own infrastructure, not rely on cloud computing and other bullshit, but have our own thing.

JULIAN: But we may have this domination of technique. If it's a fact that it's easier to use Twitter than start your own Twitter; if it's a fact that it's easier to use Facebook than DIASPORA, or some alternative; if it's a fact that cloud computing is cheaper, then these techniques and services will dominate.[78] It's not a matter of saying that we should start our own local services, because these local services simply will not be competitive, and they will only ever be used by a small minority of people. We need something better than saying that we should have a poor-man's version of Facebook and expect people to use it.

ANDY: Well, coming back to the Catholic Church, we're going back to times where there is one major issuer of books, as Amazon is trying to control the complete supply chain of e-books, so we must keep our own printing/publishing capabilities. This might sound a bit over-reaching, but we have seen what these companies can do if they or the governmental agencies they depend on in their jurisdiction don't want stuff to be happening. And I think the next step will obviously have to be that we need our own money, so that even if they don't like the fact that we support projects like WikiLeaks or whatever, we have our own way to do that without relying on a central infrastructure which all goes through one jurisdiction.

JÉRÉMIE: I would like to agree with Andy. I think that architecture matters and this is central to everything we stand for. But this is a message that we have a responsibility to convey to the public, because we understand it, as hackers, as technicians who build the internet every day and play with it. And maybe this is a way to win the hearts and minds of the younger generations. I think this is why the copyright wars are so essential, because with peer-to-peer technologies, since Napster in 1999, people just understood—got it—that by sharing files between individuals…

JULIAN: You're a criminal.

JÉRÉMIE: No, you build better culture.

JULIAN: No, you're a criminal.

JÉRÉMIE: That's the storytelling, but if you build a better culture for yourself, everybody will use Napster.[79]

ANDY: The history of the human race and the history of culture is the history of copying thoughts, modifying and processing them further on, and if you call it stealing, then you're like all the cynics.

JÉRÉMIE: Exactly, exactly! Culture is meant to be shared.

JULIAN: Well, in the West since the 1950s we've had industrial culture. Our culture has become an industrial product.

JÉRÉMIE: We are feeding the troll here because he's playing the devil's advocate and he's doing it very well.

JACOB: I'm not biting. It's such obvious bullshit.

JÉRÉMIE: It is bullshit. In the political storytelling it is called stealing, but I want to make my point that everybody who used Napster back in 1999 became a music fan and then went to concerts and became a descriptor telling everybody, "You should listen to those people, you should go to that concert" and so on. So people have had a practical example of how peer-to-peer technology decentralized the architecture. Actually, Napster was a bit centralized back at that time, but it seeded the idea of a decentralized architecture. Everybody had a concrete example where a decentralized architecture brought good to society, and when it is about sharing culture it is exactly the same as when it is about sharing knowledge. Sharing of knowledge is what we're talking about when we're discussing routing around censorship, or cutting through the political storytelling to build a better democratic system and to make society better.

So, we have examples where decentralized services and sharing between individuals makes things better, and the counter-example is the devil's advocate Julian is playing, where an industry comes and says, "Oh, this is stealing and this is killing everybody, killing actors, killing Hollywood, killing cinema, killing kittens and everything." They have won battles in the past and now we may be about to win the ACTA battle. And I once again have to disagree with the devil's advocate Julian was playing earlier. ACTA has been the greatest example of the circumvention of democracy so far, of sitting on the face of parliament and the international institutions, sitting on the face of public opinion and imposing unacceptable measures through the back door. If we manage to kick that out, then we will set a precedent, then we will have an opportunity to push for a positive agenda, to say, "ACTA is over, now let's go and do something that really goes in the favor of the public." And we're working towards that and some members of the European Parliament now understand that when individuals share things, when they share files without a profit, they shouldn't go to jail, they shouldn't be punished. I think that if we manage that one we have a strong case for exposing to the rest of the world that the sharing of knowledge, the sharing of information, makes things better, that we have to promote it and not fight it, and that any attempt—whether it's legislative or from a dictator or from a company—to hurt our ability to share information and share knowledge in a decentralized way must be opposed period. I think we can build momentum.

JULIAN: What about the PIPA/SOPA debate in the US? This is new legislation proposed in the US Congress to create financial embargoes and internet blockades on behalf of US industries.

JACOB: It was created specifically to attack WikiLeaks and WikiLeaks-related or WikiLeaks-like things that exist.

JULIAN: In Congress the banking blockade against us was specifically mentioned as an effective tool.[80]

JÉRÉMIE: And it was about giving this tool to Hollywood.

JULIAN: So we had a big community campaign against it and eventually Google and Wikipedia and a bunch of others joined that campaign.

But I didn't go, "Ok, that's great, we've won that battle." That scared the hell out of me, because Google suddenly saw itself as a political player and not just a distributor, and it felt that tremendous, enormous power over Congress.

JÉRÉMIE: Google was just one bit of the anti-SOPA and PIPA coalition.

JACOB: Yes, but hang on, Tumblr, I think, made more of an impact than Google did.

ANDY: Tumblr and Wikipedia and tons of individual actions, very small actions you may never have heard of, made an impact. There were thousands of them being parallelized—going in the same direction—and that's, again, decentralized political action. It's a decentralized political movement that we have witnessed. Google may have been the biggest actor that you've noticed among the others.

JULIAN: Well, it's what Congress said that it noticed.

JACOB: I take a little bit of an issue with what Jérémie said earlier because you essentially promote the idea of a political vanguard. I don't think you meant to do that but you did, and I just wanted to stop you right there, because the peer-to-peer movement is explicitly against a political vanguard. It's the idea that we are all peers and we can share between each other; we may provide different services or we may provide different functionality. Once Ross Anderson said to me, "When I joined the peer-to-peer movement fifty years ago," which

I thought was a fantastic opener. He explained that he wanted to ensure that we never un-invented the printing press. Because as we start to centralize services, as we start to centralize control of information systems, we actually do start to un-invent the printing press in the sense that the *Encyclopedia Britannica* no longer prints books and they only print CDs—if you don't have a general-purpose computer that can read those CDs, you don't have access to that knowledge. Now, in the case of the *Encyclopedia Britannica* it doesn't matter because we have Wikipedia and we have a lot of other material. But I don't think as a society that we're ready.

ANDY: I'm not sure Wikipedia is all that good compared as a resource. I don't trust a single page there that I didn't re-write myself.

JACOB: But the *Encyclopedia Britannica* is no different. It's just one source of many, and what matters is the verification of the data. All I mean to say is that we should not promote this idea of a vanguard because it is very dangerous.

JULIAN: Hang on, why? I'm a bit of a vanguard. What's the problem with them?

JÉRÉMIE: I'm not talking about vanguards, I'm just saying that we have new tools between our hands. We were mentioning the printing press. Another visionary, a friend of mine Benjamin Bayart, maybe less well-known in the non-French speaking world, said, "The printing press taught the people how to read; the internet taught the people how to write."[81] This is something very new, this is a new ability for everyone to be able to write and express themselves.

ANDY: Yes, but filtering is becoming even more important these days.

JÉRÉMIE: Sure because everybody talks, and many people say bullshit. As the academic and activist Larry Lessig and, I guess, so many other teachers will tell you, we teach people how to write but when students give in their papers, ninety-nine point something per cent of them are crap, but nevertheless we teach them how to write.[82] And so, of course, people say bullshit on the internet—that's obvious. But to be able to use this ability to express yourself in public makes you more and more constructed in your way of speaking over time, more and more able to participate in complex discussions. And all the phenomena we're describing are built around engineered complexity that we need to break down into small parts in order to be able to understand and debate calmly. It's not about a political vanguard, it's about channeling through the political system this new ability to express ourselves that we all have between our hands, to share our thoughts, to participate in the sharing of knowledge without being a member of a political party, of a media company, or of whatever centralized structure you needed in the past in order to be able to express yourself.

THE INTERNET AND ECONOMICS

JULIAN: I want to look at three basic freedoms. When I interviewed the head of Hezbollah, Hassan Nasrallah...

JACOB: Where's that fucking drone strike? What's that up there?

JULIAN: Well, he has his own kind of house arrest as well because he can't leave his secret location.

JACOB: I'm not sure that I would make that comparison. Please don't make that comparison.

JULIAN: There's a question whether Hezbollah has the ingredients of a state—has it actually become a state? This is something that is mentioned in the US embassy cables, that Hezbollah has developed its own fiber optic network in south Lebanon.[83] So, it has the three primary ingredients of a state—it has control over armed force within a particular region, it has a communications infrastructure that it has control over, and it has a financial infrastructure that it has control over. And we can also think about this as three basic liberties. The liberty of freedom of movement, physical freedom of movement—your ability to travel from one place to another, to not have armed force deployed against you. We can think about the liberty of freedom of thought, and freedom of communication, which is inherently wrapped up in freedom of thought—if there's a threat against you for speaking publicly, the only way to safeguard your right to communicate is to communicate privately. And finally, the freedom of economic interaction, which is also coupled, like the freedom of communication, to the privacy of economic interaction. So let's speak about these ideas that have been brewing in the cypherpunks since the 1990s of trying to provide this very important third freedom, which is the freedom of economic interaction.

JÉRÉMIE: But why would you need only three freedoms? In my European Charter for Fundamental Rights there are more.

JULIAN: Privacy becomes important either from a communitarian perspective, which is you need privacy in order to communicate freely and to think freely, or you need it for your economic interaction in some way. So I think there are more derivative freedoms but these—the first three that I said—are the fundamental freedoms from which other freedoms derive.

JÉRÉMIE: Well, there is a legal definition to fundamental freedom.

JULIAN: But I've read the EU Charter and I can tell you that it's an absolute dog's breakfast of consensus.

JÉRÉMIE: Yes, OK, and the lobbies managed to put intellectual property in the EU Charter.

JULIAN: All sorts of crazy, crazy things.

ANDY: I do think there is a point that we can agree on, which is that the money system, the economic infrastructure to interchange money, totally sucks at the moment. And even anybody who just has an eBay account will wildly agree with that, because what Paypal is doing, what Visa and MasterCard are doing, is actually putting people in a de facto monopoly situation. There was this very interesting thing from the WikiLeaks cables also, that said that the Russian government tried to negotiate a way that Visa and MasterCard payments from Russian citizens within Russia would have to be processed in Russia, and Visa and MasterCard actually refused it.[84]

JULIAN: Yes the power of the US embassy and Visa combined was enough to prevent even Russia from coming up with its own domestic payment card system within Russia.

ANDY: Meaning that even payments from Russian citizens within Russian-to-Russian shops will be processed through American data centers. So the US government will have jurisdictional control, or at least insight.

JULIAN: Yes, so when Putin goes out to buy a Coke, thirty seconds later it is known in Washington DC.

ANDY: And that, of course, is a very unsatisfying situation, independent of whether I like the US or not. This is just a very dangerous thing to have a central place where all payments are stored, because it invites all kinds of usage of that data.

JACOB: One of the fundamental things the cypherpunks recognized is that the architecture actually defines the political situation, so if you have a centralized architecture, even if the best people in the world are in control of it, it attracts assholes and those assholes do things with their power that the original designers would not do. And it's important to know that that goes for money.

JULIAN: Like oil wells in Saudi Arabia as well, the curse of oil.

JACOB: No matter where we look we can see, especially with financial systems, that effectively even if the people have the best of intentions, it doesn't matter. The architecture is the truth. It's the truth of the internet with regard to communications. The so-called lawful intercept systems, which is just a nice way of saying spying on people…

JULIAN: It's a euphemism, lawful interception.

JACOB: Absolutely, like lawful murder.

ANDY: Or lawful torture.

JACOB: You've heard about the lawful drone strikes on American citizens by the US president, Obama? When he killed

Anwar al-Awlaki's sixteen-year-old son in Yemen that was lawful murder, or targeted killing as they put it.[85] So-called lawful intercept is the same thing—you just put lawful in front of everything and then all of a sudden because the state does it, it is legitimate. But in fact it's the architecture of the state that allows them to do that at all, it's the architecture of the laws and the architecture of the technology, just as it's the architecture of financial systems.

What the cypherpunks wanted to do was to create systems that allow us to compensate each other in a truly free way where it is not possible to interfere. Like Chaumian currencies, which are electronic currencies designed according to the specifications of David Chaum, the originator of eCash (a fully anonymous electronic currency), although you could argue that they are more centralized than is necessary. The idea is to be able to create anonymous currencies, as opposed to Visa/MasterCard, which is a tracking currency. While built around a central authority, Chaumian currencies use cryptographic protocols invented by David Chaum in order to ensure anonymous transactions.[86]

JULIAN: So, basically electronic cash but without, say, serial numbers on the cash.

JACOB: Or serial numbers that allow you to establish that it is valid currency but don't allow you to know that Julian paid Andy, or what the amount was necessarily.

JÉRÉMIE: It's recreating cash in the digital world, actually.

JULIAN: Creating an electronic currency is a big deal precisely because control over the medium of exchange is one of the three ingredients of a state, as I was saying with regard to Hezbollah. If you take away the state's monopoly over the means of economic interaction, then you take away one of the three principal ingredients of the state. In the model of the state as a mafia, where the state is a protection racket, the state shakes people down for money in every possible way. Controlling currency flows is important for revenue-raising by the state, but it is also important for simply controlling what people do—incentivizing one thing, disincentivizing another thing, completely banning a certain activity, or an organization, or interactions between organizations. So, for example, with the extraordinary financial blockade against WikiLeaks, it's not the free market that has decided to blockade WikiLeaks, because it's not a free market—government regulation has made particular financial players kings and doesn't allow other market entrants. Economic freedom has been impinged by an elite group that is able to influence both regulation and the principles involved in these banks.[87]

ANDY: Sad to say, this is the unsolved problem of the electronic world right now. Two credit companies, both with a US based electronic infrastructure for clearance—meaning access to the data in the US jurisdiction—control most of the credit card payments of the planet. Companies like Paypal, which is also governed under US jurisdiction, apply US policies, be it blocking the sale of Cuban cigars from German online retailers or the blockade of payments to WikiLeaks in non-US jurisdictions. This means the US government has access to data and the option to impose payment controls on worldwide payments.

While American citizens might argue that this is the best democracy money can buy, for European citizens this is just priceless.

JULIAN: In our traditional world we have had to a degree freedom of movement, not so great in some cases.

JACOB: Are you sure, Julian? I feel like your freedom of movement is a classic example of how free we really are.

JULIAN: Well no, the UK has announced it's going to put 100,000 people per year in my condition.[88] So I think that is collateral to a degree.

JACOB: This is the reason why the founders of my country shot people from Britain. There's a reason we shot the British. And it still exists today! The tyranny exists.

JÉRÉMIE: Let's not get personal.

ANDY: What your country, the US, is currently doing is privatizing prisons and negotiating contracts that guarantee a 90 per cent filling rate to the private companies running these former US government prisons.[89] Well, what is that? That is capitalism as absurd as it can get.

JULIAN: There are more people in US prisons than there were in the Soviet Union.

JACOB: This is this fallacy where, because I object to something that is wrong you can suggest that I am part of something that is equally wrong. I'm not suggesting that the United States is perfect. I think the United States is actually pretty great in a lot of ways, but specifically with regard to the Founding Fathers' rhetoric.

JULIAN: The Founding Fathers' rhetoric is in clear dissolution in the past ten years.

JACOB: We must not forget that a lot of perception about the Founding Father's rhetoric is mythology and we should be cautious about idolizing them. So, yes, of course. All I mean to say by my comment about British tyranny and the situation that Julian finds himself in is that this is actually a cultural thing. This is where society comes in and where society is very important, and it's very difficult for the technology to supplant that. And financial issues are the most dangerous thing to be working on. There is a reason why the person that created another electronic currency, Bitcoin, did so anonymously. You do not want to be the person that invents the first really successful electronic currency.[90]

JULIAN: The guys who did e-gold ended up being prosecuted in the US.[91]

JACOB: It's so incredibly frustrating.

JULIAN: I want to go back to these three fundamental freedoms: freedom of communication, freedom of movement and freedom of economic interaction. If we look at the transition of our global society onto the internet, when we made that transition the freedom of personal movement is unchanged essentially. The freedom of communication is enhanced tremendously in some ways, in that we can now communicate to many more people; on the other hand it is also tremendously degraded because there is no privacy anymore, and so our communications can be spied on, and are spied on and stored and, as a result, can be used against us. And so that elementary interaction that we have with people physically is degraded.

ANDY: Privacy is available but it comes at a cost.

JULIAN: Our economic interactions have suffered precisely the same consequences. So in a traditional economic interaction, who knows about it? The people who saw you go down to the market. Now, who knows about your economic interaction? If you buy something from your next-door neighbor with your Visa card, which you could have done in a traditional market society almost completely privately, who knows about it now?

JACOB: Everybody.

JULIAN: Everybody knows. They have the data sharing between all the major Western powers, they all know about it and they store it forever.

ANDY: Julian, it's not wrong what you're saying, but I'm not sure you can really distinguish between the freedom of communication and the freedom of economic interaction, because the internet as we have it today is the infrastructure for our social, our economic, our cultural, our political, all our interactions.

JACOB: Certainly the freedom of movement.

ANDY: Whatever the communication architecture is, the money is just bits. This is just a usage of the internet. So if the economic system is based on the electronic infrastructure, the architecture of the electronic infrastructure says something about how the money flow is going, how it is being controlled, how it is being centralized and so on. The internet was perhaps not even thought to be the infrastructure for everything in the first days but the economic logic said, "Well, it's cheaper to do that with the internet." The banks and credit card companies previously had ATM machines out there with X.25 interfaces, which was a separate network ten or twenty years ago, and now it's all TCP/IP because it is cheaper.[92] So the architecture of the technology is becoming a key issue because it affects all the other areas, and that's what we need to actually rethink, meaning that if we want a decentralized economic way of handling our payments, we need to take the infrastructure in our hands.

JACOB: Bitcoin is essentially an electronic currency.

ANDY: With no inflation.

JACOB: It tends to do it in a decentralized manner, so instead of having the Federal Reserve you have a bunch of people all across the world that together agree on what reality is, and what their current currency is.

JULIAN: And there are some computer programs that help facilitate this.

JACOB: I want to explain it in a non-technical manner. It's an electronic currency which is more like a commodity than a currency in that people do determine how many euros it is to one Bitcoin. So it's a little bit like gold in this regard and there's a cost of the so-called mining of the Bitcoins, where you do a search on a computer to find a Bitcoin, and the idea is that there's this computational complexity and it's tied to the value of the thing. So in non-technical terms it's a way for me to send Julian currency and for Julian to confirm it without Andy really being able to interfere or to stop it. There are some problems, though—it's not actually an anonymous currency, and this is a really bad thing in my opinion.

JULIAN: Bitcoin is a very interesting hybrid, as the account holders are completely private and you can create an account at will, but the transactions for the entire Bitcoin economy are completely public. And that is how it works; it needs to be that way in order for everyone to agree that a transaction has occurred, that the sending account now has less money and the destination that much more. That's one of the few ways to run a distributed currency system that doesn't require a central server, which would be an attractive target for coercive control. It is the distribution that is really innovative in Bitcoin, and the algorithms that permit that distribution, where you do not trust any particular part of, if you like, the Bitcoin banking network. Rather the trust is distributed. And enforcement is not done through law or regulation or auditing, it is done through the cryptographic computational difficulty that each part of the network has to go through to prove that it is doing what it claims. So the enforcement of honest Bitcoin "banking" is built into the architecture of the system. Computation translates into electricity costs for each branch of the Bitcoin bank, so we can assign a cost to commit fraud, in terms of electricity prices. The work needed to commit a fraud is set to be higher in electricity costs than the economic benefit derived from it. It is very innovative, not because these ideas haven't been explored before (they have been for over twenty years on paper), but because Bitcoin got the balance almost right and added one very innovative idea about how to prove a true global consensus about transactions of the Bitcoin economy, even assuming that many banks were fraudulent and that anyone could start one.

Of course, just like every other currency, you have to buy the currency with something else; with work, or Bitcoins are traded for another currency—there are foreign exchange groups that do that. There are some other limitations. It has about a ten minute settlement time—it takes about ten minutes of computational work between handing over currency and the other party being sure that there is a global consensus that the transaction has taken place. It is exactly like cash, so it has all the theft problems that cash has. It has all the benefits as well: once you've got it you're sure that you have been paid, the check can't be cancelled, the bank can't retract it. Coercive force relations cut their ties. On the other hand, you have to guard cash well. That is, I think, its biggest problem. But it is quite easy to build additional layers on top, to build escrow services where you store your Bitcoins in a service that is specifically designed to keep them safe and add insurance against theft.

JACOB: Interestingly, if the people that created Bitcoin had made it mandatory to use Tor, so you don't create an account, you create some cryptographic identifiers, it would have been possible if everything went over Tor as a core design that you did have location anonymity, even if you had long-term identifiers that identified you so you could link your transactions together.

JÉRÉMIE: Without entering into the technical considerations we could agree that Bitcoin has excellent concepts but some flaws. It has a deflationist nature, because money tends to disappear from Bitcoin. So it cannot work in the long run but it sets concepts that can be improved. It is maybe version 0.7 or 0.8 now.

JACOB: This is like David Chaum reinvented.[93]

ANDY: Bitcoin was the most successful attempt to introduce a digital currency for the last ten years, I would say.

JULIAN: They got the balance almost right. I think Bitcoin will continue. It's an efficient currency; you can start up an account in ten seconds, and to transfer money there is no overhead other than the cost of an internet connection and a few minutes of electricity. It's highly competitive compared to almost any other form of currency transfer. I think it will prosper. Look at what happened following several Bitcoin thefts and negative follow-up press in the summer of 2011 that drove the exchange rate down to three dollars US.[94] Bitcoin has gradually risen back up to twelve dollars. It hasn't climbed up or bounced back suddenly, it has climbed up in a gradual curve that seems to show a broad demand for the currency. I suspect a lot of the demand is petty drug trading, mail order marijuana and so on.[95] But Bitcoin has low overheads as a currency. Several ISPs, especially in places that can't get easy credit-card services, like the former Soviet Union, are starting to use it.

There will be a crackdown if it continues to grow. That will not get rid of Bitcoin, because cryptography prevents any simple attack via coercive force from working, but the sort of foreign exchange services that convert to and from Bitcoin could be targeted much more easily. On the other hand, these exchanges can run anywhere in the world, so there are quite a few jurisdictions one has to work through before there are no more exchanges, and then the black market has its own exchange logic. I think the play that needs to be conducted with Bitcoin is to get it adopted by the ISP and internet service industry for these little games you buy on Facebook and so on, because it is so efficient, and once it is well adopted by a variety of industries they will form a lobby to stop it being banned. That's a bit like how cryptography was adopted. It used to be classified as arms trading, and some of us as arms traders, but once it was in browsers and used for banking there was a powerful enough lobby to prevent it from being banned—although I concede there are moves afoot again.

JACOB: The problem is that the privacy concerns are wrong. Let's be honest here. It's wrong to suggest that the economics of the situation are different with the internet than without the internet. When I came here and I bought British pounds I had to give up my social security number, which is my unique identifier in the United States, I had to give up my name, I had to link it to a bank account, I had to give them the money. They recorded all the serial numbers and then they took all that information and they reported that to the Federal Government. So, that's the analogue. It's actually harder to get foreign currencies in the US because we're so far away from everywhere else. But there's a historical trend of control with regard to currency and it's not just in regard to the internet that we see this control. In fact, there are to my understanding ATM machines in banks that record the serial numbers of cash and then track them to do flow analyses on the cash to see where it has been spent and who has done stuff with it.

If we look at those systems and then we look at the internet, they did not improve the privacy as we migrated to the internet—in fact, they kept it as bad as it was to begin with. In this way I think it's very important to then look at the trends from the world before the internet to see where we're headed. What we find is that if you have a lot of money you can pay a premium to keep your privacy, and if you don't have a lot of money you almost certainly have no privacy. And it's worse with the internet. Something like Bitcoin is a step in the right direction because when combined with an anonymous communications channel, like Tor for example, it allows you to actually send WikiLeaks a Bitcoin over Tor and anyone watching this transaction would see a Tor user sending a Bitcoin and you receiving it. It's possible to do it—that is much better in some ways than cash.

JULIAN: We all speak about the privacy of communication and the right to publish. That's something that's quite easy to understand—it has a long history—and, in fact, journalists love to talk about it because they're protecting their own interests. But if we compare that value to the value of the privacy and freedom of economic interaction, actually every time the CIA sees an economic interaction they can see that it's this party from this location to this party in this location, and they have a figure to the value and importance of the interaction. So isn't the freedom, or privacy, of economic interactions actually more important than the freedom of speech, because economic interactions really underpin the whole structure of society?

JACOB: They're inherently linked. I think you can tell the difference between the American and European cypherpunks right here because most of the American cypherpunks would say that they are exactly the same. Because in a society which has a free market one would argue that you put your money where your mouth is.

JULIAN: Where you put your money is where you put your power.

JACOB: Exactly. I'm not saying that that is right, that's almost a Right attitude towards this, which maybe is not what we want. Maybe we want a socially constrained capitalism, for example.

JULIAN: If we just look from a simple intelligence perspective: You've got a 10 million dollar intelligence budget. You can spy on people's email interactions or you can have total surveillance of their economic interactions. Which one would you prefer?

ANDY: Well, these days they will say, "Ok, we'll just force the payment companies and banks to use the internet, so we have both." And that's what they did. So the point is indeed that there is no direct escape here. You can do things like use Tor to protect your communication, you can encrypt your phone calls, you can do secure messaging. With money, it's a lot more complicated and we have these things called money laundering laws and so on, and they tell us that drug and terrorist organizations are abusing the infrastructure to do evil things.

JACOB: It's the Horsemen of the Info-pocalypse.

ANDY: Actually, I'd be very interested to have more transparency on surveillance companies and government spending on these issues. The question is what do we buy when we provide total anonymity of only the money system? What would actually happen? I think this might lead here and there to interesting areas where people may get themselves a little more easy and say, "Well, you know, I can raise my voice, I can go to the parliament, but I can also just buy some politicians."

JÉRÉMIE: You're describing the US, right?

JACOB: It's not anonymous.

ANDY: I'm not sure this is limited to the US. In Germany we don't actually call it corruption, we call it foundations that buy paintings painted by wives of politicians, and so it's in the art trade or other areas. So we have better names for it. Maybe in France you call it friendship parties and others call it hiring prostitutes.

JÉRÉMIE: In the US it's particular because the link between the political system and money is so tight. Larry Lessig said, after ten years of working on copyright issues, that he gave up on trying to fix copyright (he didn't really give up) because he found out that the problem wasn't politicians' understanding of what a good copyright policy would be, the problem was that there were just too many links to the industrial actors that were pushing for a bad copyright regime.[96] So there is a real problem here.

JULIAN: Are you sure it's a problem, Jérémie? Maybe in fact it is a good attribute that those industries that are productive...

ANDY: I think the devil's advocate is drinking my whiskey.

JACOB: Let's see if he can actually finish this sentence without cracking up. Troll us, Master Troll.

JULIAN: Those industries that are productive, that produce wealth for the whole society, use a portion of their money in order to make sure that they continue to be productive, by knocking out random legislation that comes out of political myth-making seeded by hype. And the best way to do that is, in fact, to buy Congressmen, to take the labor of their productive industry and use it to modify the law—so as to keep the productive nature of the industry going.

JACOB: Wait—I'll get this one. Ready? Ready? Right now, ready? No.

JULIAN: Why?

JACOB: There are a couple of reasons but for one, there is a feedback loop that is extremely negative. For example, I believe one of the largest political campaign donors in the state of California is the prison guard union, and part of the reason for this is because they like to lobby for stronger laws, not because they care about the rule of law but because there is a job incentive.[97] So, if you see that these people are lobbying to create more prisons, to jail more people, to have longer sentences, what is it they are effectively doing? What they're doing is they're using the benefit that they receive for the labor that was actually beneficial—arguably—in order to expand the monopoly that the state grants to them.

JULIAN: So they're just using it for wealth transfer from actual productive industries to industries that are not productive?

JACOB: You could sum it up that way.

JULIAN: But maybe that's just a small component. Every system is abused, perhaps these free-riders that are just involved in wealth transfer are a small element, and in fact the majority of the lobbying, the majority of the influence on Congress does actually come from productive industries making sure that that the laws continue to permit those industries to be productive.

JACOB: But you can measure that very easily because you can look to see which people wish to promote rent-seeking activities, and wish to restrict the freedoms of other people to create a situation in which they themselves could not have risen to be where they are today. When they do those things then you know that something has gone wrong and they're just protecting what they have, which they've essentially created through an exploitation—usually by an appeal to emotion where they say, "Gosh, stop the terrorist, stop the child pornography, stop the money laundering, fight the war on drugs." Maybe those things are all totally reasonable in the context in which they're originally presented, and usually they are, because generally speaking we think that those are bad because there is a serious component in each one of them.

ANDY: I'd like to get back to copyright and give you another example—there were serious issues when cars came out. Those who ran companies transporting passengers with horses feared that this would kill their business, which was true, but maybe it also made sense. I was invited to speak to the German movie companies' association and before my speech there was a professor from a university in Berlin who spoke super politely about the evolution of the human race and the development of culture, saying that copying thoughts and processing them further on is the key thing, just as making movies is about taking themes and expressing them in a dramaturgic way. After his forty minutes the moderator brashly interrupted him and said, "Ok, so after you just said that we should legalize theft, let's see what the guy from the Chaos Computer Club has to say." And I was thinking, "Wow, what the fuck? If I'm going to speak out, will they let me out of here alive?" So some industries just have business cases that are not serving evolution. This is selfish, staying on their de-evolutionary drive, making it even more monopolistic. When cassettes came out they also thought that the record industry was going to die. The opposite happened, the record industry exploded. The question is what's the policy here? What's the positive way we could formulate these things?

JULIAN: I just wonder whether we couldn't, in fact, standardize the actual practice in the United States, and formalize it so you do simply buy Senators and buy votes in the Senate.

JÉRÉMIE: No, no, no, no.

ANDY: Let's assume we have the money.

JULIAN: Yes, and that it is all open and there are buyers and each one goes to an auction.

ANDY: But the weapons industry would still have more money.

JULIAN: No, I think it wouldn't. I actually think the military-industrial complex would be relatively marginalized because their ability to operate behind closed doors in a system that is not open to general market bidding is in fact higher than other industries.

JACOB: There's a fundamental inequality in the system.

JÉRÉMIE: From an economic liberal, anti-monopolistic perspective, when you say let's let the dominant actors decide what the policy will be, I can answer you with the experience of the internet in the last fifteen years, where innovation was so-called bottom up, where new practices emerged out of nothing, where a couple of guys in a garage invented a technology that spread.

JULIAN: For nearly everything, for Apple, for Google, for YouTube, for everything.

JÉRÉMIE: For everything. Everything that happened on the internet just boomed after being unknown a few months or a few years before, so you cannot predict what the next innovation will be and the pace of innovation is so fast that it is much faster than the policy-making process.

So when you design a law that has an impact on what the market is today, on what the strength relationship between various companies and actors is, if you strengthen one that is strong already you may stop a new entrant from appearing that would have been more efficient.

JULIAN: The market has got to be regulated to be free.

JÉRÉMIE: Of course you have to fight monopolies and you need to have a power that is superior to the power of those companies in order to punish bad behavior—but my point here is that policy has to adapt to society, and not the other way around. We have the impression with the copyright wars that the legislator tries to make the whole of society change to adapt to a framework that is defined by Hollywood, say. "Ok, what you're doing with your new cultural practice is just morally wrong, so if you don't want to stop it then we'll design legal tools to make you stop doing what you think is good." This is not the way to make good policy. A good policy looks at the world and adapts to it in order to correct what is wrong and to enable what is good. I'm convinced that when you enable the most powerful industrial actors to decide what policy should be, you don't go that way.

ANDY: I'm just trying to positively get us into thinking what would be a good policy. What you just formulated is at this stage, for me, a little too complicated. I'm trying to simplify a little bit. There is this guy called Heinz von Foerster—the godfather of cybernetics—who once made a set of rules and one of the rules was, "Always act in a way that increases the options."[98] So with policies, technology, whatever, always do what gives you more, not less options.

JULIAN: Chess strategy as well.

ANDY: It was mentioned that the increase of privacy on money transactions might have a negative effect, so we need to think, "The money system right now has a specific logic and the question is how do we exclude the money system from taking over other areas?" Because the money system has the ability—unlike the communication sector—to affect and totally limit the options of people in other areas. If you can hire contract killers to do specific things, or if you can buy weapons and engage in a war with other countries, then you're limiting other people's option to live, to act. If I put more money in communications then more people have more options. If I put more weapons on the market...

JACOB: No—the more you have the ability to surveil, the more you have control.

ANDY: Which is another good argument for restricting the weapons market, including telecommunication surveillance technology.

JACOB: Sure, you want to restrict my ability to sell that, how do you do that? How do you restrict my ability to transfer wealth?— Also through communications networks. One of the most offensive things about the bailouts in the United States—which were offensive for a whole bunch of reasons to many people—was that they showed that wealth is just a series of bits in a computer system. Some people by begging in a very effective way managed to get many of the bits to be set high, and then what is the question? Is there value in the system if you can just cheat the system and get your bits set high? And everybody else who is struggling to get along isn't acknowledged as even having bits that are worth flipping in the first place.[99]

ANDY: So what you're saying is we need a totally different economic system? Because value today is not attached to economic value.

JACOB: No, I'm saying there is an economic value.

ANDY: You can do bad things and generate money with it, and you can generate good things and you will not get a cent.

JACOB: Well no, what I'm saying is you can't decouple the economy from communication. I'm not talking about whether or not we need a different economic system. I'm not an economist. I'm just going to say that there is some value in the communication systems and in the freedom of those communications, just as there is value in the freedom of actual bartering—I have the right to give you something in exchange for your labor, just as I have the right to explain an idea and you have the right to tell me what you think of my idea. We can't say that the economic system exists in some kind of vacuum. The communication system is directly tied together with this, and this is part of society.

If we are going to have this reductionist notion of freedom, of the three freedoms Julian mentioned, this is obviously tied to freedom of movement—you cannot even buy a plane ticket now without using a trackable currency, otherwise you're flagged. If you walk into an airport and you try to buy a ticket on the same day with cash, you're flagged.

You get extra security searches, you cannot fly without identification and if you were to be so unlucky as to buy your plane ticket with a credit card they'll log everything about you—from your IP address to your browser. I actually have the Freedom of Information Act data for my Immigration and Customs Enforcement records from a couple of years ago, because I thought someday maybe it would be interesting to look at the differences. And sure enough it has Roger Dingledine, who bought me a plane ticket for some work thing, his credit card, his address where he was when he bought it, the browser that he used and everything about that plane ticket was all put together.

JULIAN: And that went to the US government, it wasn't just kept in the commercial processor?

JACOB: Right. The commercial data was collected, sent to the government and they were tied together. And the thing that I find to be really crazy is that it's essentially the merging of these three things you're talking about. It was my right to travel freely, it was my ability to buy that plane ticket or for someone else to purchase that plane ticket, and it was the ability for me effectively to be able to speak—I was going to travel to speak somewhere, and in order to do that I had to make compromises in the other two spheres. And in fact it impacts my ability to speak, especially when I find out later what they have collected and that they've put it together.

CENSORSHIP

JULIAN: Jake, can you speak a little bit about the detainment that you've had at US airports, and why that has occurred?

JACOB: They've asserted that it occurs because "I know why."

JULIAN: But they don't say?

ANDY: Can I try to summarize it, because technical security and the security of governmental affairs are two things that are totally detached. You can have a totally secure technical system and the government will think it's no good, because they think security is when they can look into it, when they can control it, when they can breach the technical security. This was not about Jake trying to approach planes, to kill anybody, to hijack the plane or whatever. This was about his ability to affect governmental affairs by travelling to other countries, speaking to people, and spreading ideas. That is the most dangerous thing that happens to governments these days—when people have better ideas than what their policy is.

JACOB: I totally appreciate you complimenting me there in that statement, but I would just like to point out that this is way worse than that, because this is the data they collect on everyone. This was before I did anything interesting at all; it was merely the fact that I was travelling and the systems themselves, the architecture, promoted this information collection. This is before I was ever stopped for anything, it was before I was deported from Lebanon, it was before the US government took a special interest in me.

ANDY: Maybe they forecast it, maybe they saw it earlier than you did.

JACOB: Of course they did, partially because of collecting this data. But they always give me different answers. Usually they say one response, which is, uniformly across the board, "Because we can." And I say, "Ok, I do not dispute your authority—well, I do dispute your authority, I do not dispute it now—I merely wish to know why this is happening to me." Now people tell me all the time, "Well, isn't it obvious? You work on Tor," or, "You're sitting next to Julian, what did you expect?" It's fascinating to me because each of the different people that are holding me—usually from the Customs and Border Protection and Immigration and Customs Enforcement in the United States—will tell me it is because they have the authority to do so more than anything else. I've also had them tell me bullshit like, "Oh, remember 9/11? That's why," or, "Because we want you to answer some questions and this is the place you have the least amount of rights, or so we assert."

And in this situation they'll deny access to a lawyer, they'll deny access to a bathroom but they'll give you water, they will give you something to drink, like a diuretic, in order to convince you that you really want to co-operate in some way. They did this to pressure, for political reasons. They asked me questions about how I feel about the Iraq War, how I feel about the Afghan War. Basically, every step of the way they repeated the tactics of the FBI during COINTELPRO (the massive domestic covert operations program that ran between 1956 and 1971). For example, they specifically tried to assert their authority to change political realities in my own life, and to try to pressure me not only to change them, but to give them some special access to what's going on in my head. And they've seized my property. I'm not really at liberty to discuss all of the things that have occurred to me because it's a very murky grey area where I don't really know whether or not I'm even allowed to talk about them. I'm sure this happened to other people but I've never heard of it happening to them.

I was in the Toronto Pearson airport once while travelling home from an event where I was visiting my family. I was travelling back to Seattle, where I was living at the time, and they detained me, they put me in the secondary screening, and then the tertiary screening, and then finally into a holding cell. And they held me for so long that when I was finally released I missed my flight. But there's a curious thing, which is that these pre-detention areas are actually technically US soil on Canadian soil, and so they have a rule that says that if you miss your flight or it's so long before the next flight, you have to leave. So I technically got kicked out of America by being detained so long and I had to enter Canada, fly across the country, rent a car, and then drive across the border. And when I got to the border they said, "How long have you been in Canada?" and I said, "Well, five hours plus the detainment that happened in Toronto," so I had been in Canada about eight hours, and they said, "Well, come on in, we're going to detain you again." And then they ripped my car apart and they took my computer apart and they looked through all this stuff, and then they held me. They gave me access to a bathroom within half an hour, they were very merciful you could say. And this is what they call the border search exception—this kind of behavior is because they have the ability, they assert, to do this, and no one challenges them about it.[100]

JULIAN: So, this has happened to you, but Chinese people I speak to, when they speak about the great firewall of China—in the West we talk about this in terms of censorship, that it's blocking Chinese citizens from coming out and reading what is said about the Chinese government in the West and by Chinese dissidents and by the Falun Gong and by the BBC and, to be fair, in actual propaganda about China—but their concern is actually not about censorship. Their concern is that in order to have internet censorship there must also be internet surveillance. In order to check what someone is looking at, to see whether it is permitted or denied, you must be seeing it, and therefore if you are seeing it you can record it all. And this has had a tremendous chilling effect on the Chinese—not that they're being censored but that everything that they read is being spied upon and recorded. In fact, that's true for all us. This is something that modifies people, when they are aware of it. It modifies their behavior and they become less resolute in complaining about various kinds of authorities.

JACOB: That's the wrong answer to that type of influence, though. Their harassment of me at borders, for example, is not unique, in that every Arab-American, since September 11th and before, has had to deal with this. It's just that I refuse to let the privilege of having white skin and a US passport go to waste in this, and I refuse to be silent about it because the things that they are doing are wrong, and the power that they are using, they are abusing. And we must stand up to those things, just in the same way that there are brave people in China that stand up to this, like Isaac Mao for example.[101] He has been working very strongly against this type of censorship effectively, because the right answer is not to just give in to this type of pressure merely because the government asserts that it has the ability to do this.

JÉRÉMIE: But once again we're talking politics because what you say is, basically, that people should stand up for their rights—but people should understand why to do so, and then have the ability to communicate between each other to do so. I had the occasion to talk with some people from China—and I don't know if they were in some position in the state, or if they were selected in order to be able to go outside to talk to me—but when talking to them about internet censorship I very often had this answer: "Well, it's for the good of the People. There is censorship, yes, because if there wasn't censorship then there would be extremist behavior, there would be things that we would all dislike, and so the government is taking those measures in order to make sure that everything goes well."

JACOB: That's the same argument for organ harvesting. Don't let those organs go to waste!

JÉRÉMIE: If you look at the way Chinese censorship is being done, you see from the technical perspective that it's one of the most advanced systems that exists in the world.

JACOB: Absolutely.

JÉRÉMIE: And I've heard that on Weibo—that is the Chinese equivalent of Twitter—the government has the ability to filter some hashtags to make sure they don't leave a selected province.

JACOB: It's crucial to remember that when people talk about censorship in Asia they like to talk about it in terms of the "the other"—as if it only affects the people in "OverThereIstan." It's very important to know that when you search on Google in the United States, they say that they have omitted search results because of legal requirements. There is a difference between the two—both in how they are implemented and, of course, in the social reality of the how, the why, and the where even—but a big part of that actually is the architecture. For example, over the American internet, it's very decentralized—it's very hard to do the Chinese-style censorship in the same respect.

JULIAN: Well, a big chunk of it is Google and you can censor Google. There are a load of pages that reference WikiLeaks that are censored by Google.

JACOB: Yes, no doubt. And actually since the index itself is free, it's possible to do a differential analysis.

JULIAN: Yes, in theory.

JACOB: In theory. And in practice there are some people that are working on that type of censorship detection by looking at the differences from different perspectives in the world. I think that it is important to remember that censorship and surveillance are not issues of "other places"—people in the West love to talk about how "Iranians and the Chinese and North Koreans need anonymity and freedom, but we don't need it here." And by "here," they usually mean "in the United States." But actually it is not just oppressive regimes, because if you happen to be in the top echelon of any regime it's not oppressive to you. But we consider the UK to be a wonderful place; generally people think Sweden is a pretty great place, and yet you can see that when you fall out of favor with the people in power you don't end up in a favorable position. But Julian's still alive, right? So clearly that's a symbol that it's a free country—is that right?

JULIAN: I worked hard to maintain my current position. But maybe we should speak about internet censorship in the West. This is very interesting. If we go back to 1953 and we look at the great Soviet encyclopedia, which was distributed everywhere, that encyclopedia sometimes had amendments as politics changed in the Soviet Union. In 1953 Beria, the head of the NKVD, the Soviet secret police, died and fell out of political favor and so his section, which described him in glowing terms, was removed by the encyclopedia authority which posted out an amendment that was to be pasted into all of those encyclopedias. It was extremely obvious. I'm mentioning this example because it was so obvious and so detectable that the attempt became part of history. Whereas in the UK we have the *Guardian* and the other major newspapers ripping out stories from their internet archives in secret without any description. You go to those pages now and you try to find them, for example stories on the fraud case of the billionaire Nadhmi Auchi, and you see, "Page not found," and they have also been removed from the indexes.

Let me tell you my involvement with the Nadhmi Auchi story. In 1990 Iraq invaded Kuwait, and that led to the first Gulf War. The Kuwaiti government in exile, and also during its return, needed cash, so it started to sell off various assets including several oil refineries outside Kuwait. A UK businessman, Nadhmi Auchi, who had immigrated to the UK in the early 1980s from Iraq, where he used to be a figure in Saddam Hussein's regime, was a broker in that deal and was subsequently accused of being involved in channeling $118 million of illegal commissions. That investigation was the largest corruption investigation in European postwar history. In 2003 Auchi was convicted of fraud in what was to become known as the Elf Aquitaine scandal. Nevertheless, nowadays he has over 200 companies registered through his Luxembourg holding outfit, and others through Panama. He is involved in post-war Iraqi cellular contracts and many other businesses around the world.[102]

In the United States Tony Rezko, a fundraiser for Barack Obama's Senate campaign, was a long term pal of Auchi's, who had been his financier. Similarly Auchi and Rezko became involved with the former Governor of Illinois, Rod Blagojevich. Both Rezko and Blagojevich were convicted of corruption, Rezko in 2008 and Blagojevich in 2010/11 (after the FBI recorded him in telephone intercept trying to sell Obama's former Senate seat). In 2007/8, when Obama was running to be the Democrats' presidential candidate, the US press started to investigate Obama's connections. They investigated Rezko and reported some links in relation to the purchase of Barack Obama's house. In 2008, shortly before his trial, Rezko received a $3.5 million transfer from Auchi which he didn't report to the court, despite being required to—for which he was jailed. So US press scrutiny turned to Auchi, and at that moment he instructed UK lawyers Carter-Ruck to wage an aggressive campaign on much of the 2003 reportage about the Elf Aquitaine scandal and his conviction in France. This was very successful. He targeted the UK press, and even US blogs, and had nearly a dozen articles removed that we know about. Most of those articles, including in UK newspaper archives, simply disappeared. It was as if they had never even existed. There was no, "We have received a legal complaint and decided to remove the story." They also disappeared from the indexes. WikiLeaks dug these out and republished them.[103]

JACOB: They erase history.

JULIAN: History is not only modified, it has ceased to have ever existed. It is Orwell's dictum, "He who controls the present controls the past and he who controls the past controls the future." It is the undetectable erasure of history in the West, and that's just post-publication censorship. Pre-publication self-censorship is much more extreme but often hard to detect. We've seen that with Cablegate as WikiLeaks works with different media partners all over the world, so we can see which ones censor our material.[104]

For example the *New York Times* redacted a cable that said that millions of dollars were distributed to covertly influence politically connected Libyans via oil companies operating in Libya. The cable didn't even name a specific oil company—the *New York Times* simply redacted the phrase "oil services companies."[105] Probably the most flagrant was the *New York Times'* use of a sixty-two-page cable about North Korea's missile program, and whether they had sold missiles to the Iranians, from which the *New York Times* used two paragraphs in order to argue, in a story, that Iran had missiles that could strike Europe, whereas elsewhere in the cable just the opposite was argued.[106]

The *Guardian* redacted a cable about Yulia Tymoshenko, the former prime minister of Ukraine, which said that she might be hiding her wealth in London.[107] It censored out allegations that the Kazakhstani elite in general was corrupt—not even a named person—and an allegation that both ENI, the Italian energy company operating in Kazakhstan, and British Gas were corrupt.[108] Essentially the *Guardian* censored instances where a rich person was accused of something in a cable, unless the *Guardian* had an institutional agenda against that rich person.[109] So, for example, in a cable about Bulgarian organized crime there was one Russian, and the *Guardian* it made it look like the whole thing was about him, but he was just one person on a long list of organizations and individuals associated with Bulgarian organized crime.[110] *Der Spiegel* censored out a paragraph about what Merkel was doing—no human rights concern whatsoever, purely political concerns about Merkel.[111] There are lots of examples.[112]

ANDY: Our understanding of freedom of information and the free flow of information is in some way a very radical new concept if you look at planet Earth. I would say it's not much different between Europe and other countries. Well, there are countries that have a democratic framework, which means you can read and understand and maybe even legally fight the censorship infrastructure, but it doesn't mean it's not there, while you will have a hard time trying in Saudi Arabia or China.

JULIAN: My experience in the West is that it is just so much more sophisticated in the number of layers of indirection and obfuscation about what is actually happening. These layers are there to give deniability to the censorship that is occurring. You can think about censorship as a pyramid. This pyramid only has its tip sticking out of the sand, and that is by intention. The tip is public—libel suits, murders of journalists, cameras being snatched by the military, and so on—publicly declared censorship. But that is the smallest component. Under the tip, the next layer is all those people who don't want to be at the tip, who engage in self-censorship to not end up there. Then the next layer is all the forms of economic inducement or patronage inducement that are given to people to write about one thing or another. The next layer down is raw economy—what it is economic to write about, even if you don't include the economic factors from higher up the pyramid. Then the next layer is the prejudice of readers who only have a certain level of education, so therefore on one hand they are easy to manipulate with false information, and on the other hand you can't even tell them something sophisticated that is true. The last layer is distribution—for example, some people just don't have access to information in a particular language. So that is the censorship pyramid. What the *Guardian* is doing with its Cablegate redactions is in the second layer.

Now, such censorship is deniable because it either it takes place out of the light, or because there is no instruction to censor a particular claim. Journalists are rarely instructed, "Don't print anything about that," or, "Don't print that fact." Rather they understand that they are expected to because they understand the interests of those they wish to placate or grow close to. If you behave you'll be patted on the head and rewarded, and if you don't behave then you won't. It's that simple. I'm often fond of making this example: the obvious censorship that occurred in the Soviet Union, the censorship that was propagandized about so much in the West—jackboots coming for journalists in the middle of the night to take them from their homes—has just been shifted by twelve hours. Now we wait for the day and take homes from journalists, as they fall out of patronage and are unable to service their debts. Journalists are taken from their homes by taking homes from the journalists. Western societies specialize in laundering censorship and structuring the affairs of the powerful such that any remaining public speech that gets through has a hard time affecting the true power relationships of a highly fiscalized society, because such relationships are hidden in layers of complexity and secrecy.

ANDY: Jérémie mentioned the pedo-Nazis.

JACOB: We're back to the pedo-Nazis again.

JÉRÉMIE: Two Horsemen in one.

ANDY: The pedo-Nazis pretty well summarized the German, or maybe part of the European censoring arguments. Germany didn't want any hate speech-like content on the internet due to its history and, of course, if you tell people you need to restrict the internet because of pedophiles then you will be able to do anything. Also, there was an internal working paper of the European Commission about data retention that argued, "We should talk more about child pornography and then people will be in favor."[113]

JULIAN: Can you speak to this a little bit? That if we are to censor just one thing, say just child pornography, then in order to censor child pornography from people seeing it we need to surveil everything that everyone is doing. We need to build that infrastructure. We need to build a bulk spying and censorship system to censor just one thing.

ANDY: It's in the detail of the mechanics—the so-called pre-censorship system in Germany obliges you to name the legally responsible person for whatever you publish. So, roughly, if you publish something, be it on a piece of paper or on the internet, without saying who is legally responsible for the content, you already violate the law. This means that you allocate the responsibility and if someone violates the law by distributing, let's say child porn or hate speech, you could just say, "Ok, we look at where that guy is located and we catch him and we get the stuff off of the net."

JULIAN: That is we censor the publisher instead of censoring the reader.

ANDY: Yes. And this is watching specific things. I could agree that not everything needs to be available at all times because if I look at hate speech issues there are sometimes things with private addresses of people and so on that might lead to situations I'm not in favor of.

JULIAN: But Andy, this is such a German thing. In order to do that, in order to determine what's going to be acceptable and what's not you have to have a committee, you have to have appointments to that committee, you have to have a process of appointments to that committee...

ANDY: Yes, we have all that bullshit. The German killings in the Second World War—everything the Nazis did, every property they seized, they gave a receipt, they made a list. It was all bureaucratic acts. You can say that Germans unjustifiably killed a lot of people— that's true—but they did it in a bureaucratic manner. That's Germany.

JULIAN: If you have someone deciding what should be censored and what should not then you have to have two things. First of all, you have to build a technical architecture to do the censorship. You have to build a nationwide censorship machine to do it effectively. And then secondly, you have to have a committee and a bureaucracy to censor. And that committee inherently has to be secret because it's completely useless unless it is secret and therefore you have secret justice.

ANDY: You know what? We have one good principle in Germany.

JACOB: Just the one?

ANDY: The principle is that if it is unrealistic for a law to be applied, then it shouldn't be there. If a law doesn't make sense, like if you forbid windmills or whatever, then we say, "Hey, come on, forget it." We here are inspired by the internet as we knew it when it was growing up, by the free flow of information, in the sense of free as in unlimited, as in not blocked, not censored, not filtered. So if we apply our understanding of the free flow of information to planet Earth—and it has been roughly applied to planet Earth—we see, of course, the governments being affected by it and the way power has been applied and the way censorship has been run, be it pre-censorship, post-censorship or whatever censorship. We have all learned about these complicated conflicts that arise. The question is what is our concept of government or the future of a Post-Governmental Organization—maybe WikiLeaks is the first or one of the first PGOs—because I'm not sure governments are the right answer to all the problems on this planet, like environmental issues.

JULIAN: The governments are not sure either, of the barrier between what is government or not. It's fuzzed out now. Governments occupy space, but WikiLeaks occupies part of the space of the internet. Internet space is embedded in real space, but the degree of complexity between the embedded object and the embedding means that it's not easy for the embedding to tell that the embedded object is even part of it. So that's why we have this sense of a cyberspace—that it is actually some other realm that exists somewhere—it's because of the degree of its indirection, complexity and universality. When you read some file on the internet in one location it's the same as reading it in another location or in the future—that's its universality. So to that degree, as an organization that occupies cyberspace and is adept at moving its information around the underlying embeddings, maybe we are a post-state organization because of the lack of geographic control.

I don't want to take this analogy too far, because I am under house arrest. The coercive force of states obviously applies to all our people, wherever they are known. But the rest of the press likes to say we're a stateless media organization and they are quite right about the importance of statelessness. I always used to say, "Well what do you think Newscorp is? It's a big multinational." But nonetheless, Newscorp is structured in such a way that you can get at its key components, and that's why it has had so much trouble here in the UK with the phone-hacking scandal, and why it is trying so hard to suck up to the US establishment. But if an organization's assets are primarily its information, then it can be transnational in a way that is quite hard to stop as a result of cryptography. There is a reason a financial blockade was erected against us—our other organizational facets are harder to suppress.[114]

JACOB: If we're talking about it in Utopian terms, we have to actually go back a little bit further. So, you asked me about the harassment I received, you asked about censorship in the West and I talked earlier about Obama's targeted killing program, which they say is lawful because there is a process, therefore it counts as due process.

JULIAN: Well, a secret process.

JACOB: We can also tie this back to John Gilmore. One of John Gilmore's lawsuits about his ability to travel anonymously in the United States resulted in the court literally saying, "Look, we're going to consult with the law, which is secret. We will read it and we will find out when we read this secret law whether or not you are allowed to do the thing that you are allowed to do." And they found when they read the secret law that, in fact, he was allowed to do it, because what the secret law said did not restrict him. He never learned what the secret law was at all and later they changed the US Transportation Security Administration and Department of Homeland Security *policies* in response to him winning his lawsuit, because it turns out the secret law was not restrictive enough in this way.[115]

JULIAN: So they made it more restrictive?

JACOB: Effectively, through enabling legislation of the bureaucracy. But it's important to note that the targeted assassination program, the harassment that people face at borders, the censorship that we find online, the censorship that corporations perform at the behest of a government or at the behest of a corporation, these things all tie back together. And what it really comes down to is that the state has too much power at each of the places that we see these things come out. This is because the power has concentrated in these areas and it has attracted people that abuse it, or that push for its use. And even if there are sometimes legitimate cases, what we see is that the world would be better off if there was not that centralization, if there was not the tendency towards authoritarianism.

The West is not in any way special with regard to this, because it turns out that if you have a czar of cyber-security, well, that's not so different from a tsar that was in the internal security forces of another nation fifty years ago. We're building the same kind of authoritarian control structures, which will attract people to abuse them, and that's something that we try to pretend is different in the West. It's not different in the West because there's a continuum of governance, which is authoritarianism to libertarianism. I don't mean it in the American political party sense, but in this sense: on that continuum, the United States is very far from the USSR in many, many ways but it's a lot closer to the USSR than Christiania is, the autonomous neighborhood in the heart of Copenhagen, in Denmark.[116] And it is even further, I think, from a potential Utopian world if we went and created a brand new colony on Mars. We would want to move what we might build on Mars as far away from totalitarianism and authoritarianism as we could. These are failings when we don't have that.

JÉRÉMIE: Once again, all those topics are bound together. When we talk about concentrating power we once again talk about architecture. And when we talk about internet censorship, it is about centralizing the power to determine what people may be able to access or not, and whether government censorship or also private-owned censorship is undue power. We have this example: our website laquadrature.net got censored in the UK by Orange UK for several weeks. It was among a list of websites that Orange was denying to those less than eighteen years old.

Maybe we mentioned the term child pornography while we were opposing that type of legislation, or maybe they just disliked us because we oppose their policy against net neutrality, as we advocate for a law to ban them from discriminating their users' communications.[117] We will never know. But we have a private actor here that, as a service, was offering to remove from people the ability to access information on the internet. I see a major risk here beyond the power we give to either Orange or the Government of China or whoever.

JACOB: Clarification—when you say private in the UK, do you mean that they actually own every line, every fiber connection and everything, or do you use some of the state's resources? How were the airwaves licensed? There's no state involvement at all? They have no duty of care?

JÉRÉMIE: There is licensing. Whether it's government or company, they are changing the architecture of the internet from one universal network to a Balkanization of small sub-networks. But what we are discussing since the beginning are all global issues, whether we're talking of the financial system going awry, whether we're talking of corruption, whether we're talking about geopolitics or energy or the environment. All of these are global problems that mankind is facing today and we still have one global tool between our hands that enables better communication, better sharing of knowledge, better participation in political and democratic processes. What I suspect is that a global universal internet is the only tool we have to address those global issues and that is why this fight for a free internet is the central fight that we all here have a responsibility to fight.

ANDY: I totally agree that we need to ensure that the internet is understood as a universal network with free flow of information; that we need to not only define that very well, but also to name those companies and those service providers who provide something they call internet which is actually something totally different. But I think we have not answered the key question beyond this filtering thing. I want to give you an example of what I think we need to answer. Some years ago, about ten years ago, we protested against Siemens providing so-called smart filter software. Siemens is one of the biggest telcos in Germany and a provider of intelligence software. And they actually sold this filtering system to companies so that, for example, employees couldn't look at the site of the trade unions to inform themselves of their labor rights and so on. But they also blocked the Chaos Computer Club site which made us upset. They designated it as "criminal content" or something, for which we brought legal action. But at an exhibition we decided to have a huge protest meeting and to surround Siemens' booths and filter the people coming in and out. The funny thing was that we announced it on our site to attract as many people as possible through the internet, and the people in the Siemens booth had no fucking clue because they also used the filter software so they couldn't read the warning that was obviously out there.

JULIAN: The Pentagon set up a filtering system so that any email sent to the Pentagon with the word WikiLeaks in it would be filtered. And so in the case of Bradley Manning, the prosecution, in attempting to prosecute the case, of course, was mailing people outside the military about "WikiLeaks," but they never saw the replies because they had the word "WikiLeaks" in them.[118] The national security state may eat itself yet.

ANDY: Which brings us back to the really basic question: is there something such as negative-effecting information? So, from a society point of view, do we want a censored internet because it's better for society or not? And even if we talk about child pornography you could argue, "Wait a moment, this child pornography highlights a problem, that is the abuse of children, and in order to solve the problem we need to know the problem."

JACOB: So it provides evidence for the crime.

JULIAN: Well, no it provides a lobby.

ANDY: That would be the most radical approach but if we talk about Nazis or whatever, you still have to say what we're talking about. People who have family will ask themselves: "Well, isn't it better for society to filter the bad things out so that we stick to the good things, or is that not limiting our ability to view the problems and manage them and handle them and take care of them?"

JÉRÉMIE: I think the solution is always another one than censorship. When we talk about child pornography we shouldn't even use the word pornography—it is a representation of crime scenes of child abuse. One thing to do is to go to the servers, to disable the servers, to identify the people who uploaded the content in order to identify the people who produced the content, who abused the children in the first place. And whenever there is a network of people, a commercial network and so on, go and arrest the people. And when we pass laws—and we have one in France where you have an administrative authority from the Ministry of Interior that decides which websites will be blocked—we remove an incentive to the investigative services to go and find the people who do the bad stuff by saying, "Oh, we just remove the access to the bad stuff," like we put a hand in front of the eyes of someone looking at the problem, therefore we solved the problem. So, just from that perspective, I think it is enough to describe it like this—where we all agree that we should remove those images from the internet.

JACOB: I'm sorry, I'm squirming over here. It's so frustrating to hear the argument that you're making. I want to throw up, because what you just did, is you said, "I want to use my position of power to assert my authority over other people, I want to erase history." Maybe I'm an extremist in this case—and in many other cases, I'm sure—but I'm going to go out on a limb here. This is actually an example of where erasing history does a disservice. It turns out that with the internet we learned that there's an epidemic in society of child abuse. That's what we learned with this child pornography issue—I think it's better to call it child exploitation—we saw evidence of this. Covering it up, erasing it, is, I think, a travesty because, in fact, you can learn so much about society as a whole. For example, you can learn—and I'm obviously never going to have a career in politics after I finish this sentence, but just to be clear about this—you learn, for example, who is producing it, and you learn about the people that are victimized. It is impossible for people to ignore the problem. It means that you have to start searching out the cause that creates this, which is the exploiters of the children. Ironically some surveillance technology might be useful here in facial recognition of people and by looking at the metadata in the images. Erasing that, making sure that we live in a world where it's possible to erase some stuff and not other stuff, creating these administrative bodies for censorship and for policing—that's a slippery slope which, as we have seen, has turned directly to copyright, it has turned to many other systems.

Just because it is a noble cause to go after that, maybe we should not take the easy way out, maybe in fact we should try to solve crimes, maybe in fact we should try to help those that are victimized, even though there is a cost to that kind of helping. Maybe instead of ignoring the problem, we should look at the fact that society as a whole has this big problem and it manifests on the internet in a particular way.

It's like, for example, how when Polaroid built the Swinger camera (this instant camera for taking pictures) people started to take abusive pictures with those as well. But the answer is not to destroy a medium, or to police that medium. It is when you find evidence to prosecute the crimes that the medium has documented. It is not to weaken that medium, it is not to cripple society as a whole over this thing. Because here we talk about child pornographers, let's talk about the police. The police on a regular basis in many countries abuse people. There are probably more abusive cops on the internet than there are child pornographers on the internet.

JULIAN: There are almost certainly more.

JACOB: We know there's "n" number of policemen in the world and we know there's "x" number of those policemen that have committed ethical violations—usually violent violations. If we look at just the Occupy movement, for example, we see this. Shall we censor the internet because we know some cops are bad? Shall we cripple the police's ability to do good policing work?

JULIAN: Well, there is a question about re-victimization, which is where the child later on, or as an adult, or its social contacts, see the child abuse images again.

JACOB: As long as those cops are online, I am being re-victimized.

JULIAN: You could say seeing an image of you being beaten by a policeman is re-victimization. I would say that the protection of the integrity of the history of what actually happened in our world is more important; that re-victimization does occur, but nonetheless to set up a censorship regime which is capable of removing chunks of history means that we cannot address the problem because we can't see what the problem is. In the 1990s I acted in an advisory capacity on internet matters to pedophile-busting cops in Australia, the Victorian Child Exploitation Unit. Those cops were not happy about filtering systems, because when people can't see that there's child pornography on the internet it removes the lobby that ensures that the cops have the funds to stop the abuse of children.

JÉRÉMIE: The point on which we agree—I think it's the most important one—is that in the end it's the individual responsibility of the people who do the content, the child abuse material and things like that, that really matters and on which cops should work.

JACOB: We don't agree. That's not what I said.

JULIAN: No, Jérémie is talking about doing, not publishing—there's a difference.

JACOB: The production of the content is not the issue, actually. Just a minor clarification—if, for example, you have abused a child and Andy took a picture of this as proof, I don't think Andy should be prosecuted.

JÉRÉMIE: No, it's the people who abuse. Come on, it's aiding and abetting.

ANDY: But some people abuse the child to produce the pictures, right?

JACOB: Of course they do.

ANDY: There might also be an economic aspect involved here.

JACOB: I agree with that entirely, I'm making a distinction here, which is to say that if the content itself is a historical record which is evidence of a crime, it is evidence of a very serious crime, and we should never lose sight of the fact that there is re-victimization, but there is the original victimization and that is actually the core issue, whether or not there are pictures of it.

JÉRÉMIE: Of course. That's what I mean.

JACOB: Whether or not there are pictures is almost irrelevant. When there are pictures, it is very important to remember that you have to keep your eye on the prize, and that the goal is to actually stop the harm, stop the abuse. A big part of that is making sure that there is evidence and that there is the incentive for the people with the right tools to solve those crimes. That, I think, is incredibly important, and people really lose sight of that because the easy thing to do is to pretend that it doesn't exist, and then to stop it and say that has stopped the abuse. And it hasn't.

ANDY: And the trouble is that right now a lot of people will obviously favor the easy solution because it's very inconvenient to look at what's really going on in society. I think you do have a chance to handle a political problem because you're not trying to make a policy that ignores the problem or makes it invisible. In a way this may be cyber politics, but this is also a question of how a society handles issues, and I do have strong doubts that there is something such as information that does harm directly. It has to do with the ability to filter, of course, and it's also true that I don't want to see all the pictures that are available on the internet. There are some that I really find disgusting and distracting but the same is true for the next video store, showing movies that are fictional and ugly. So, the question is do I have the ability to handle what I'm seeing and what I'm processing and what I'm reading? And that is the filtering approach. Actually, Wau Holland, the founder of Chaos Computer Club, said something funny: "You know, filtering should be handled in the end user, and in the end device of the end user."[119]

JULIAN: So filtering should be done by the people who receive information.

ANDY: It should be done here. Here! [Pointing to his head]

JULIAN: In the brain.

ANDY: In the end device of the end user, that's this thing you have between your ears. That's where you should filter and it shouldn't be done by the government on behalf of the people. If the people don't want to see things, well, they don't have to, and you do have the requirement these days to filter a lot of things anyhow.

PRIVACY FOR THE WEAK, TRANSPARENCY FOR THE POWERFUL

JULIAN: Andy, I spoke recently with the president of Tunisia and I asked him about what was going to happen to the intelligence records from the rule of the dictator Ben Ali—the equivalent of the Stasi archives of Tunisia—and he said that while these were very interesting, the intelligence agencies are a problem, they are dangerous, and he would have to knock them off one by one. But in relation to these archives, he thought it best for the cohesion of Tunisian society that they all be kept secret so there wasn't a blame game. You were a young man during the fall of the Stasi in East Germany, can you speak a little bit about the Stasi archives, and what do you think about this opening up of security archives?

ANDY: Germany probably has the most well-documented intelligence agency on the planet, or one of them. All the documents from the East German Staatssicherheit—all the handbooks, procedural papers, training documents, internal studies—are roughly public. Roughly means that not all of them are easy to access but a lot of them are, and the government has created an agency to take care of the records so German citizens also have the right to view their own Stasi files.

JULIAN: The German government created the BStU (the Bundes-beauftragte für die Stasi-Unterlagen), this big Stasi archives file distributor.

ANDY: Yes, and journalists can apply so-called research inquiries, which is maybe comparable to freedom of information requests, to allow them to study matters. And there are lots of books, and also handbooks of strategic behavioral learning of how the Stasi applied this and that. Actually, I think this is a very good thing to learn from. I can understand it is a bit too much to expect the Tunisians to pub-lish all the personal records that the former intelligence agency made because the president—the current president—will have to judge about his own records here, and also those of his allies and so on. These intelligence agencies don't respect privacy so you will have personal records of your sexual matters, your telecommunications, your money transfers, of everything you have done, which you might not want to have disclosed.

JULIAN: Did you follow the situation with the Amn El Dawla in Egypt, the domestic state security? Thousands of people went in, they looted the archives as the Amn El Dawla tried to burn them and destroy them and dump them in the garbage, and lots of material came out and was spread around the place. You could buy a record for $2 in a local market and upload it. It hasn't destroyed Egyptian society.

ANDY: No, I'm just saying that I do have a bit of an understanding that people don't want their personal records to be released. I can understand that, if I was living in a country where forty years of intelligence was kept about me and every time I go to the loo it is being recorded.

JULIAN: But there's cost-benefit analysis, right? From my perspective, once a rat, always a rat.

ANDY: Right, but the hacker ethics argument, roughly, is to use public information and protect private information or data, and I do think that if we're advocating for privacy—and we have very good reasons to do so—we shouldn't just say there's a balance of things here. We can distinguish. It's not that we have to put it all on the public.

JACOB: But there's a benefit to that secrecy that is asymmetric. Let's take a step back. You argue essentially from a completely flawed point, which is this notion that data is private when it is limited, and that's just not true. For example, in my country if a million people have a security clearance and are allowed to access that private data...

JULIAN: 4.3 million...

JACOB: How can you call that data private? The problem is that it is not truly 100 per cent secret from every person on the planet.

JULIAN: It's secret from the powerless and to the powerful.

ANDY: Yes, you're right. But if we want to open the archive entirely...

JULIAN: It has happened in some European countries.

ANDY: No. I don't know a single country where all the records have been disclosed.

JULIAN: To a greater extent than Germany, records were released, in Poland for example.

ANDY: That might be. What has happened actually, the bad side of this deal Germany has done, is that they used former officers of the East German State Security in order for the Stasi to administer not only the Stasi records but also part of the so-called "New Germany," the unified former Eastern part. There's this interesting story about a company winning the public tender to clean the building where the records were kept. That company won the tender just because they were the cheapest bidder for the same service that other companies bid for. After six years the organization keeping the records found out that they had hired a company built up by the former Eastern intelligence to clean their own records.

JÉRÉMIE: There was a report on that on WikiLeaks. I read it. It was great.[120]

ANDY: WikiLeaks published the report about exactly that, so you are right that once these records are created and they are in the hands of evil people it is hard to declare privacy.

JULIAN: We can go to a broader issue, though. The internet has led to an explosion of the amount of information that is available to the public—it's just extraordinary. The educative function is extraordinary.

On the other hand, people talk about WikiLeaks and they say, "Look, all that private government information is now public, the government can't keep anything secret." I say this is rubbish. I say that WikiLeaks is the shadow of a shadow. In fact, that we have produced over a million words of information and given it to the public is a function of the enormous explosion in the amount of secret material out there. And, in fact, powerful groups have such a vast amount of secret material now that it dwarfs the amount of publicly available material, and the operations of WikiLeaks are just a percentage fraction of this privately held material. When you look at this balance between powerful insiders knowing every credit card transaction in the world on the one hand, and on the other hand people being able to Google and search for the blogs of the world and people's comments, how do you see this balance?

ANDY: I could argue that it is good if all these records get disclosed because people will learn that if they use their credit card they leave a trace. Some people, if we explain it to them, will find this very hard to understand and very abstract. The moment they read their own records they will understand.

JULIAN: If you get your Facebook record, which has 800 MB of information about you.

ANDY: I know that after the fall of the Eastern bloc, the German Chancellor Helmut Kohl wanted to unify Germany and the Americans made a condition within the so-called 2+4 talks. They said they wanted to still keep the German telecommunications under their control, under their surveillance, and Kohl thought it was not important because he did not understand what telecommunications surveillance is. I met someone from his office team and they said they were really upset about this and they finally organized to have, like, 8,000 pages of transcripts of his phone calls that the Stasi had made rolled into his office on two small caddies. And he said, "Hey, what the fuck is that?" They said, "Oh, that's your phone calls in the last ten years, including the ones with your girlfriends and your wife and your secretary and so on." So they made him understand what telecommunication interception is. And indeed these records from this intelligence do help people to understand what the intelligence is doing. So we could argue for full disclosure and if we were to vote on that now, I wouldn't be sure if I would really oppose it.

JULIAN: I don't want to talk about that so much, as obviously there are cases where if you're investigating the mafia, during the period of investigation you should keep the record secret. There are circumstances where this could be seen as legitimate. I'm not saying that as a policy it's legitimate; I'm saying that it's politically inevitable. There are such politically cogent demands for it—like, "these guys have murdered before, they're plotting another murder"—that regardless of whether you think that interception should be available or not, it's going to happen. You can't win that political fight. But this kind of tactical surveillance has the benefit that it can be partly regulated and the harm can be confined to a minimum number of people. When tactical interception is used for law enforcement (as opposed to intelligence) often it is part of evidence collection. The evidence ends up in court cases, and therefore it ends up public. So you have some oversight, at least some of the time, of what's going on. And you can interrogate people on the stand about how that information was collected and why we should assume it was valid. You can keep an eye on it. But regulation of strategic interception is completely absurd. It is, by definition, intercepting everyone, so what legislation are we going to apply if your starting premise is to intercept everyone?

JÉRÉMIE: This debate about full disclosure makes me think of the group known as LulzSec, who released 70 million records from Sony—all the users' data from Sony—and you could see all the addresses, email addresses and passwords. I think there were even credit card details from 70 million users. As a fundamental rights activist I thought, "Wow, there is something wrong here if to prove your point or to have fun you disclose people's personal data." I was very uncomfortable with seeing people's email addresses on the record. In a way, I thought those people were having fun with computer security, and what they were demonstrating is that a company as notorious and powerful as Sony wasn't able to keep its users' secrets secret, and having those 70 million users search in a search engine for their email address or for their name and find this record would make them instantly realize, "Oh wow, what did I do when I disclosed this data to Sony? What does it mean to give personal data to a company?"

JACOB: Then they shoot the messenger.

RATS IN THE OPERA HOUSE

JULIAN: We've gone through all these pessimistic scenarios, so now I want to look at a potential Utopian scenario. We have the radicalization of internet youth, and now internet youth is approaching the majority of youth. On the other hand, we have some desperate attempts at anonymization and freedom of publication, freedom from censorship—we have a vast array of state and private sector interactions which are fighting against that—but let's assume that we take the most positive trajectory. What does it look like?

JACOB: I think we need the right to read and the right to speak freely without exception for every single person, not one single human being excepted, no exceptions whatsoever, to misquote Bill Hicks.[17] He talked about this with regard to education, clothing and food, but that's really what it comes down to: everyone has the right to read, everyone has the right to speak freely. In that comes a right to anonymous speech, the ability to be able to pay people in a way where there is no interference from third parties, the ability to travel freely, the ability to correct data about you that is in systems. To have transparency and accountability for any systems where we see any sort of agency.

ANDY: I would add the thought that with the increase of information processing systems and the network side of it, and with the availability of tools like Tor and encryption and so on, the amount of data that can be suppressed is pretty low, meaning that governments need to just do that and they know it. They know that acting in secret these days just means acting for a matter of time in secret, it will be subject to public record sooner or later, and this is a good thing. This changes the way they act. This means they know there is accountability. This also means they actually force whistleblowing inside processes, like in the Sarbanes-Oxley Act requiring companies which are registered in the US stock markets to have a whistleblower infrastructure, so that people who need to report criminal or other misbehavior by their superiors have a way to report it without being affected directly by those they are reporting on.[122] So this is a good thing and this will bring more sustainable processes in the long term.

JÉRÉMIE: Adding to what Jake just said, I think we must make it clear for everyone that a free, open and universal internet is probably the most important tool that we have to address the global issues that are at stake, that protecting it is probably one of the most essential tasks that our generation has between its hands, and that when somebody somewhere—whether it's a government or a company—restricts some people's ability to access the universal internet, it is the whole internet that is affected. It's the whole of humanity that is being restricted. As we are witnessing that we can collectively increase the political cost of taking this decision, all of the citizens accessing the free internet can deter that behavior. We are beginning to see that as network citizens we have power in political decisions and we can make our elected representatives and our governments more accountable for what they do when they make bad decisions that affect our fundamental freedoms and that affect a free global universal internet.

So I think we should practice that. We should continue to share knowledge about how to do it. We should continue to improve our ways of action, the way we exchange tactics about going to the parliament, about exposing what the politicians are doing, about exposing the influence of industry lobbies on the policy-making process. We should continue to build tools to make citizens more able to build their own decentralized encrypted infrastructures, to own their communication infrastructure. We should promote these ideas to the whole of society as a way to build a better world and we are beginning to do it—we should just continue.

JULIAN: Jake, if you look at people like Evgeny Morozov's description of the problems in the internet, these issues were foreshadowed long ago by the cypherpunks.[123] It wasn't a view that one should simply complain about the burgeoning surveillance state and so on, but that we can, in fact, must build the tools of a new democracy. We can actually build them with our minds, distribute them to other people and engage in collective defense. Technology and science is not neutral. There are particular forms of technology that can give us these fundamental rights and freedoms that many people have aspired to for so long.

JACOB: Absolutely. The key thing I think that people should walk away with—especially if there's some sixteen-year-old or eighteen-year-old person that wishes they could make the world a better place—is that nobody sitting here and nobody anywhere in the world was born with the accomplishments that they later have on their gravestone. We all build alternatives. Everybody here has built alternatives and everyone, especially with the internet, is empowered to do that for the context in which they exist. And it is not that they have a duty to do it, but it is that if they wish to do this, they can. And if they do that, they will impact many people, especially with regard to the internet. Building those alternatives has an amplification, a magnification.

JULIAN: So, just for you, if you build something you can give it to a billion people to use.

JACOB: Or if you participate in building an anonymity network—like the Tor network for example—you help to build the alternative of anonymous communication where previously it did not exist.

JÉRÉMIE: It's about sharing that knowledge freely and enabling communication channels for knowledge to flow freely, this is what you are doing. Tor is free software, it is as widely spread as it is today because we embed that notion of freedom in the way we build alternatives and build technology and build models.

JACOB: We need free software for a free world, and we need free and open hardware.

JULIAN: But by free you mean unconstrained, people can muck about with the internals, they can see how it operates?

JACOB: Absolutely. We need software that is as free as laws in a democracy, where everyone is able to study it, to change it, to be able to really understand it and to ensure that it does what they wish that it would do. Free Software, Free and Open Hardware.[124]

JULIAN: They had this notion from the cypherpunks that "code is law."

JÉRÉMIE: That's from Larry Lessig.

JULIAN: On the internet what you can do is defined by what programs exist, what programs run, and therefore code is law.

JACOB: Absolutely, and what that means is that you can build alternatives, especially in terms of programming but even in terms of 3D printing or social things like hacker spaces that exist.[125] You can help to build alternatives and the key thing is to drive them home into a normalization process, one where people become socially very used to being able to build their own three-dimensional objects, to being able to modify their own software, and where they are aware that if someone blocks them from doing that then whoever is doing the blocking isn't providing internet access, they are providing a filternet or a censornet, and, in fact, they are violating their duty of care.

That's what every single one of us has done with our lives and people should know that they have the ability to do it for future generations, and for this generation now. That's why I'm here—because if I don't support Julian now, in the things that he is going through, what kind of world am I building? What kind of message do I send when I let a bunch of pigs push me around? No way, never. We have to build and we have to change that. As Gandhi said, "You have to be the change you want to see in the world," but you have to be the trouble you want to see in the world, too.[126] That's a line from *A Softer World*, it's not the same as the Gandhi quotation, but I think people need to know that they cannot just sit idly by, they need to actually take action, and hopefully they will.[127]

ANDY: I think we're seeing a good chance that people can proceed further on from where we are, and alternatives come from people who are unsatisfied with the situation they find or the options they have.

JULIAN: Can you talk a bit about the Chaos Computer Club in this context?

ANDY: Always CCC… fnord.[128]

JULIAN: It is unique in the world, actually.

ANDY: The CCC is a galactic hacker organization that promotes freedom of information, transparency of technology, and cares about the relationship between human and technological development, so society and development interacting with each other.

JULIAN: This has actually become political.

ANDY: The CCC has become like a forum of the hacker scene with a few thousand members based a little bit in Germany—but we don't understand ourselves as living in Germany, we understand ourselves as living in the internet, which is perhaps a big part of our self-understanding which also attracts. We are very well-networked with other hacker groups in France, in America and other places.

JULIAN: And why do you think that this started in Germany? The heart is in Germany—it's expanded out to the rest of the world.

ANDY: Germans always try to structure everything.

JÉRÉMIE: German engineering is better.

JULIAN: But I think it's not just that. It's that this is Berlin and it's the fall of the East.

ANDY: It has to do with different things. Germany has done the worst thing a country can to do to others, so it is perhaps a bit more immune to doing those things again, like starting a war with other countries. We've done it all, we've been through it, we've been punished hard and we had to learn from it, and actually this decentralized thinking and anti-fascistic behavior, like avoiding a totalitarian state, is still taught in German schools because we experienced that at the worst level. So I think that is part of understanding the CCC, which is a bit of a German phenomenon. Wau Holland, the creator who founded the CCC, also had a very heavily political approach to this. I saw his father at his grave, when his son actually died before him, and his father was not saying pleasant words. He said: "...and that there will never be any totalitarian, non-peaceful activities from German ground again." That was his father's comment when he buried his son, and for me that explained a lot about why Wau was so heavily into influencing and taking care of people, acting peacefully with others, spreading ideas and not limiting them, and not behaving aggressively but co-operatively.

And the thought of co-operatively creating things—like open source movements and so on—has indeed been infecting and coming together with the thoughts of American cypherpunks and Julian Assange/WikiLeaks and so on. This is a global thing going on now, which does have very different, very decentralized cultural attitudes of Swiss, German, Italian hackers—and that is good. Italian hackers behave totally differently than German hackers—wherever they are, they need to make good food; with German hackers, they need to have everything well-structured. I'm not saying the one is better than the other, I'm just saying that each of these decentralized cultures has its very beautiful parts. At the Italian hacker conference you can go to the kitchen and you will see a wonderful place; at the German hacker camp you will see a wonderful internet, but you better not look at the kitchen. Still, the heart of it is we are creating. And I think we find ourselves in some kind of a common consciousness which is totally away from our national identity—from being Germans or from being Italians or from being Americans or whatever—we just see that we want to solve problems, we want to work together. We see this internet censorship, this fight by governments against new technology, as some kind of evolutionary situation which we have to overcome.

We are on the way to identifying solutions and not only problems, and that is a good thing. We probably still have to fight a lot of bullshit for the next I don't know how many years, but now finally there's a generation of politicians coming up who don't see the internet as the enemy but understand that it is part of the solution, and not part of the problem. We still have a world built on weapons, on the power of secret-keeping, on an entire economic framework and so on, but that is changing and I do think we are very important in the policy-making right now. We can discuss the issues in a controversial way—and that is something that the CCC has managed for a long time, actually. We are not a homogeneous group, we have very different opinions. I appreciate that we sit here together and we don't come up with the best answers right away, we just come up with questions, and we crash our different ideas on the table and see what the bottom line is. That's the process that needs to go on, and that's what we need a free internet for.

JULIAN: I posed the question of what the most positive trajectory for the future would look like. Self-knowledge, diversity, and networks of self-determination. A highly educated global population—I do not mean formal education, but highly educated in their understanding of how human civilization works at the political, industrial, scientific and psychological levels—as a result of the free exchange of communication, also stimulating vibrant new cultures and the maximal diversification of individual thought, increased regional self-determination, and the self-determination of interest groups that are able to network quickly and exchange value rapidly over geographic boundaries. And perhaps that has been expressed in the Arab Spring and the pan-Arab activism which was potentiated by the internet. In our work with Nawaat.org, who created Tunileaks, pushing the State Department cables past the regime's censorship into pre-revolutionary Tunisia, we saw first-hand the terrific power of the network for moving information to where it is needed, and it was tremendously rewarding to have been in a position, because of our efforts, to contribute to what was starting to happen there.[129] I do not perceive that struggle for self-determination as distinct from our own.

This positive trajectory would entail the self-knowing of human civilization because the past cannot be destroyed. It would mean the inability of neo-totalitarian states to arise in practice because of the free movement of information, the ability for people to speak to each other privately and conspire against such tendencies, and the ability for micro-capital to move without control away from such places which are inhospitable to human beings.

From those underpinnings you can build a wide variety of political systems. Utopia to me would be a dystopia if there was just one. I think Utopian ideals must mean the diversity of systems and models of interaction. If you look at the churning development of new cultural products and even language drift, and sub-cultures forming their own mechanisms of interaction potentiated by the internet, then yes I can see that that does open this possible positive path.

But I think in all probability tendencies to homogenization, universality, the whole of human civilization being turned into one market, mean you will have normal market factors such as one market leader, one second, a third niche player, and then stragglers that don't make any difference at all, for every service and product. I think it will perhaps mean massive language homogenization, massive cultural homogenization, massive standardization in order to make these rapid interchanges efficient. So I think the pessimistic scenario is also quite probable, and the transnational surveillance state and endless drone wars are almost upon us.

Actually I'm reminded of a time when I smuggled myself into Sydney Opera House to see Faust. Sydney Opera House is very beautiful at night, its grand interiors and lights beaming out over the water and into the night sky. Afterwards I came out and I heard three women talking together, leaning on the railing overlooking the darkened bay. The older woman was describing how she was having problems with her job, which turned out to be working for the CIA as an intelligence agent, and she had previously complained to the Senate Select Committee for Intelligence and so on, and she was telling this in hushed tones to her niece and another woman. I thought, "So it is true then. CIA agents really do hang out at the Sydney opera!" And then I looked inside the Opera House through the massive glass panels at the front, and there in all this lonely palatial refinement was a water rat that had crawled up in to the Opera House interior, and was scurrying back and forth, leaping on to the fine linen-covered tables and eating the Opera House food, jumping on to the counter with all the tickets and having a really great time. And actually I think that is the most probable scenario for the future: an extremely confining, homogenized, postmodern transnational totalitarian structure with incredible complexity, absurdities and debasements, and within that incredible complexity a space where only the smart rats can go.

That's a positive angle on the negative trajectory, the negative trajectory being a transnational surveillance state, drone-riddled, the networked neo-feudalism of the transnational elite—not in a classical sense, but a complex multi-party interaction that has come about as a result of various elites in their own national countries lifting up together, off their respective population bases, and merging. All communications will be surveilled, permanently recorded, permanently tracked, each individual in all their interactions permanently identified as that individual to this new Establishment, from birth to death. That's a major shift from even ten years ago and we're already practically there. I think that can only produce a very controlling atmosphere. If all the collected information about the world was public that might rebalance the power dynamic and let us, as a global civilization, shape our destiny. But without dramatic change it will not. Mass surveillance applies disproportionately to most of us, transferring power to those in on the scheme who nonetheless, I think, will not enjoy this brave new world much either. This system will also coincide with a drones arms race that will eliminate clearly defined borders as we know them, since such borders are produced by the contestation of physical lines, resulting in a state of perpetual war as the winning influence-networks start to shake down the world for concessions. And alongside this people are going to just be buried under the impossible math of bureaucracy.

How can a normal person be free within that system? They simply cannot, it's impossible. Not that anyone can ever be completely free, within any system, but the freedoms that we have biologically evolved for, and the freedoms that we have become culturally accustomed to, will be almost entirely eliminated.

So I think the only people who will be able to keep the freedom that we had, say, twenty years ago—because the surveillance state has already eliminated quite a lot of that, we just don't realize it yet— are those who are highly educated in the internals of this system. So it will only be a high-tech rebel elite that is free, these clever rats running around the opera house.

ENDNOTES

1. Put simply, cryptography, from the Greek for "secret writing," is the practice of communicating in code.
2. "Oxford English Dictionary Updates Some Entries & Adds New Words; Bada-Bing, Cypherpunk, and Wi-Fi Now in the OED," ResourceShelf, September 16, 2006: http://web.resourceshelf.com/go/resourceblog/43743 (accessed October 24, 2012).
3. WikiLeaks: http://wikileaks.org
4. For more on the rubberhose file see: "The Idiot Savants' Guide to Rubberhose," Suelette Dreyfus: http://marutukku.org/current/src/doc/maruguide/t1.html (accessed October 14, 2012).
5. For more on the book Underground see: http://www.underground-book.net
   For more on the movie Underground: The Julian Assange Story see the Internet Movie Database: http://www.imdb.com/title/tt2357453/ (accessed October 21, 2012).
6. Noisebridge is a San Francisco-based hackerspace, an infrastructure provider for technical-creative projects, collaboratively run by its members: https://www.noisebridge.net/wiki/Noisebridge
   Chaos Computer Club Berlin is the Berlin organization of the Chaos Computer Club (for which see below): https://berlin.ccc.de/wiki/Chaos_Computer_Club_Berlin
7. Tor Project: https://www.torproject.org
8. The Chaos Computer Club is Europe's largest hacker association. Its activities range from technical research and exploration to campaigns, events, publications and policy advice: http://www.ccc.de
9. EDRI: http://www.edri.org
10. ICANN: http://www.icann.org
11. buggedplanet: http://buggedplanet.info

12. Cryptophone: http://www.cryptophone.de
13. La Quadrature du Net: http://www.laquadrature.net
14. Collateral Murder: http://www.collateralmurder.com
    The Iraq War Logs: http://wikileaks.org/irq
    The Afghan War Diary: http://wikileaks.org/afg
    Cablegate: http://wikileaks.org/cablegate.html
15. "Congressional committee holds hearing on national security leak preven-
    tion and punishment," Reporters Committee for Freedom of the Press,
    July 11, 2012: http://www.rcfp.org/browse-media-law-resources/news/
    congressional-committee-holds-hearing-national-security-leak-prevent
    (accessed October 21, 2012).
16. For further information on the WikiLeaks Grand Jury consult free-
    lance journalist Alexa O'Brien's timeline: http://www.alexaobrien.com/
    timeline_us_versus_manning_assange_wikileaks_2012.html (accessed
    October 22, 2012).
17. "Bradley Manning's treatment was cruel and inhuman, UN torture
    chief rules," Guardian, March 12, 2012: http://www.guardian.co.uk/
    world/2012/mar/12/bradley-manning-cruel-inhuman-treatment-un
    (accessed October 24, 2012).
18. "WikiLeaks: guilty parties "should face death penalty,"" Telegraph,
    December 1, 2010: http://www.telegraph.co.uk/news/worldnews/
    wikileaks/8172916/WikiLeaks-guilty-parties-should-face-death-penalty.
    html (accessed October 22, 2012).
19. "CIA launches task force to assess impact of U.S. cables' exposure by
    WikiLeaks," Washington Post, December 22, 2012: http://www.wash-
    ingtonpost.com/wp-dyn/content/article/2010/12/21/AR2010122104599.
    html?hpid=topnews&sid=ST2010122105304 (accessed October 22,
    2012).
20. "WikiLeaks fights to stay online after US company withdraws domain
    name," Guardian, December 3, 2012: http://www.guardian.co.uk/media/
    blog/2010/dec/03/wikileaks-knocked-off-net-dns-everydns (accessed
    October 23, 2012).
21. "Don't Look, Don't Read: Government Warns Its Workers Away From
    WikiLeaks Documents," New York Times, December 4, 2010: http://
    www.nytimes.com/2010/12/05/world/05restrict.html?hp&_r=2&
    (accessed October 23, 2012).
22. "Banking Blockade," WikiLeaks: http://www.wikileaks.org/Banking-
    Blockade.html (accessed October 22, 2012)

23. Jacob's written account of his detentions is recommended reading. See: "Air Space—a trip through an airport detention center," boingboing, October 31, 2011: http://boingboing.net/2011/10/31/air-space-a-trip-through-an-ai.html.

Also of importance is an interview with Jacob about the detentions on Democracy Now. "National Security Agency Whistleblower William Binney on Growing State Surveillance," Democracy Now, April 20, 2012: http://www.democracynow.org/2012/4/20/exclusive_national_security_agency_whistleblower_william (both links accessed October 23, 2012).

24. The case is officially known as In the Matter of the 2703(d) Order Relating to Twitter Accounts: Wikileaks Rop_G IOERROR; and BirgittaJ.

25. "Secret orders target email," Wall Street Journal, October 9, 2011: http://online.wsj.com/article/SB10001424052970203476804576613284007315072.html (accessed October 22, 2012).

26. "Twitter Ordered to Yield Data in WikiLeaks Case," New York Times, November 10, 2011: https://www.nytimes.com/2011/11/11/technology/twitter-ordered-to-yield-data-in-wikileaks-case.html?_r=1 (accessed October 22, 2012).

27. "ACLU & EFF to Appeal Secrecy Ruling in Twitter/WikiLeaks Case," Electronic Frontier Foundation press release, January 20, 2012: https://www.eff.org/press/releases/aclu-eff-appeal-secrecy-ruling-twitter-wikileaks-case (accessed October 22, 2012).

28. This was the April 6, 2008 protest in support of the suppressed strike of the Mahalla al-Kobra textile workers. Shortly before the strike the "April 6 Youth Movement" was formed as a Facebook group, conceived to encourage Egyptians to hold protests in Cairo and elsewhere to coincide with the industrial action in Mahalla. The protests did not go to plan, and the Facebook group's administrators Esraa Abdel Fattah Ahmed Rashid and Ahmed Maher were arrested, along with others. Maher was tortured for his Facebook password. The April 6 Youth Movement went on to play a role in the 2011 Egyptian revolution. See "Cairo Activists Use Facebook to Rattle Regime," Wired, October 20, 2008: http://www.wired.com/techbiz/startups/magazine/16-11/ff_facebookegypt?currentPage=all (accessed October 23, 2012).

29. "How to Protest Intelligently," anonymous authors, distributed at the outset of the eighteen-day uprising that removed President Mubarak (Arabic): http://www.itstime.it/Approfondimenti/EgyptianRevolutionManual.pdf. Excerpts from the document were translated into English and published as, "Egyptian Activists' Action Plan: Translated," Atlantic, January 27, 2011:

http://www.theatlantic.com/international/archive/2011/01/egyptian-activists-action-plan-translated/70388 (both links accessed October 23, 2012).

30. The Panopticon was a prison devised by the philosopher Jeremy Bentham in 1787, designed so as to allow one prison guard to covertly surveil all prisoners at once via line of sight. Jeremy Bentham (edited by Miran Bozovic), The Panopticon Writings, (Verso, 1995), available online at: http://cartome.org/panopticon2.htm (accessed October 22, 2012).

31. Johannes Gutenberg (1398-1468) was a German blacksmith who invented mechanical movable type printing, an invention that gave rise to some of the most significant social upheaval in history. The invention of the printing press is the closest historical analogue to the invention of the internet.

32. John Gilmore is one of the original cypherpunks, a founder of the Electronic Frontier Foundation, and a civil liberties activist. The phrase cited by Andy was first quoted in: "First Nation in Cyberspace," Time Magazine, December 6, 1993. See John Gilmore's site: http://www.toad.com/gnu (accessed October 22, 2012).

33. "Proprietary technologies are any types of systems, tools, or technical processes that are developed by and for a specific business entity… [T]he ideas developed and submitted by employees are usually considered the intellectual property of the employer, thus allowing them to qualify as proprietary technology." Definition taken from wiseGEEK: http://www.wisegeek.com/what-is-proprietary-technology.htm (accessed October 22, 2012).

34. Cory Doctorow, "The coming war on general-purpose computing," boingboing, January 10, 2012 (based on a keynote speech delivered to the Chaos Computer Congress, December 2011): http://boingboing.net/2012/01/10/lockdown.html (accessed October 15, 2012).

35. Stuxnet is a highly sophisticated computer worm widely believed to have been developed by the US and Israel to attack Siemens equipment allegedly used by Iran for uranium enrichment. For an overview of Stuxnet, see Wikipedia: http://en.wikipedia.org/wiki/Stuxnet.
See also, "WikiLeaks: US advised to sabotage Iran nuclear sites by German thinktank," Guardian, January 18, 2011: http://www.guardian.co.uk/world/2011/jan/18/wikileaks-us-embassy-cable-iran-nuclear.
WikiLeaks carried one of the earliest reports of the effects now believed to have been a result of Stuxnet—the nuclear accident at Natanz nuclear facility in Iran. See, "Serious nuclear accident may lay behind Iranian nuke chief's mystery resignation," WikiLeaks, July 17, 2009: http://

wikileaks.org/wiki/Serious_nuclear_accident_may_lay_behind_Iranian_ nuke_chief%27s_mystery_resignation.

Evidence from the global intelligence company Stratfor, leaked by WikiLeaks, suggests Israeli involvement. See Email ID 185945, The Global Intelligence Files: http://wikileaks.org/gifiles/docs/185945_re-al-pha-s3-g3-israel-iran-barak-hails-munitions-blast-in.html (all links accessed October 16, 2012).

36.   Pentesting, short for penetration testing, is a security engineering term for conducting an attack in a legally authorized manner on a computer system or a computer network, as an unauthorized user might, in order to evaluate how secure it is. Security researchers are often recruited from the hacker community to conduct penetration testing on secure systems.

37.   Capture the Flag is originally an outdoor game, normally involving two teams, where both teams hold a position and guard a flag. The objective is to capture the other team's flag, and return it to base. At hacker conferences hackers play a computer-based version where teams attack and defend computers and networks.

38.   Sysadmin Cup is a contraction of System Administrator Cup. A system administrator is a person working in the IT profession who maintains and operates a computer system or network. Jacob is saying that the exercise was like a tournament for system administrators.

39.   "Aaron says encryption protects privacy, commerce," USIS Washington File, October 13, 1998: http://www.fas.org/irp/news/1998/10/98101306_ clt.html (accessed October 21, 2012).

40.   Wassenaar Arrangement website: http://www.wassenaar.org (accessed October 21, 2012).

41.   Andy is referring to various developments in the "First Crypto Wars" of the 1990s. When cypherpunk activists began to spread strong cryptographic tools as free software, the US administration took steps to prevent cryptographic tools being used effectively. It classified cryptography as a munition and restricted its export; it tried to introduce competing technologies that were deliberately broken so that law enforcement could always decrypt information; and it tried to introduce the controversial "key escrow" scheme. For a short period after the turn of the century it was widely accepted that these efforts had been comprehensively defeated. However, a "Second Crypto War" is now well underway, with legislative and technical efforts to backdoor or otherwise marginalize the use of cryptography.

42. The sample calculation was for the published 196.4 billion minutes of land-line calls in Germany in 2010, digitized with an 8 Kbps voice-codec, summing up to an amount of 11,784 Petabyte (Pb), rounded up with overhead to 15 Pb. Assuming rough storage costs of 500,000 USD (500 KUSD) for a Pb, that is 7.5 million USD or about 6 million EUR. Add costs for a decent data center setup, processing power, connections and man power. Even if all 101 billion minutes of mobile phone calls in Germany in 2010 are included, with another 50 Pb and 18.3 million EUR, the price is still less than a single military airplane like the Eurofighter (90 million EUR) or the F22 (150 million USD).

43. For more on VASTech see buggedplanet: http://buggedplanet.info/index.php?title=VASTECH (accessed October 21, 2012).

44. The NSA warrantless domestic surveillance scandal is the most consequential case of mass surveillance in United States history. The US Foreign Intelligence Surveillance Act 1978 (FISA) made it illegal for US agencies to spy on US citizens without a warrant. After 9/11, the NSA began to engage in mass violations of FISA, authorized by a secret executive order of George W. Bush. The Bush administration claimed executive authority to do this under 2001 emergency legislation passed by Congress: The Authorization for the Use of Military Force (AUMF), and the PATRIOT ACT. The NSA's warrantless domestic spying program—which involved co-operation from private companies, including AT&T—remained secret until 2005, when it was exposed by the New York Times. See "Bush Lets U.S. Spy on Callers Without Courts," New York Times, December 16, 2005: http://www.nytimes.com/2005/12/16/politics/16program.html?pagewanted=all.

    Reporters for the New York Times had been contacted by an anonymous whistleblower who had leaked the existence of the warrantless surveillance program. In 2004 the then executive editor of the New York Times, Bill Keller, agreed on the request of the Bush administration to withhold the story for a year, until after Bush was reelected. In 2005, the New York Times rushed to print the story when it learned of a possible Pentagon Papers-style prior restraint injunction being sought by the administration. The Bush administration denied that there was any illegality involved in the NSA program. The Justice Department launched an immediate investigation into the source of the leak, involving twenty-five federal agents and five prosecutors. Senior officials within the Republican Party called for the prosecution of the New York Times under the Espionage Act.

In the wake of the New York Times story other whistleblowers came forward to the press, gradually presenting a detailed picture of lawlessness and waste at the highest levels of the NSA. A host of class action lawsuits were taken by advocacy groups like the American Civil Liberties Union (ACLU) and the Electronic Frontier Foundation (EFF). In one of these cases, ACLU v. NSA, the plaintiffs were denied standing because they could not prove that they had been personally spied on. In another, Hepting v. AT&T, an AT&T whistleblower, Mark Klein, came forward with an affidavit revealing the extent of AT&T's cooperation with the domestic spying program. See the Hepting v. AT&T section on the EFF website: https://www.eff.org/cases/hepting.

Mark Klein was a witness in Hepting v. AT&T. An ex-employee of AT&T working in Folsom, San Francisco, his affidavit to the EFF in Hepting v. AT&T disclosed the existence of "Room 641A," a strategic interception facility operated by AT&T for the NSA. The facility provided access to fiber optic trunks containing Internet backbone traffic, giving the capacity to engage in surveillance of all internet traffic passing through the building, both foreign and domestic. Another NSA whistleblower, William Binney, has estimated that there are as many as twenty such facilities, all placed at key points in the United States' telecommunications network.

Klein's affidavit gives important information about the character of the NSA surveillance program, confirmed by NSA whistleblowers. This is an example of "strategic interception"—all internet traffic passing through the United States is copied and stored indefinitely. It can be known with certainty that domestic US traffic is also intercepted and stored, because, from an engineering standpoint, when dealing with this volume of traffic it is impossible to screen out traffic for which a FISA warrant would be required. Official legal interpretation of FISA now holds that an "intercept" has only occurred when a domestic communication already intercepted and stored by the NSA is "accessed" on the NSA's database, and that it is only at this stage that a warrant is required. US citizens should assume that all their telecommunications traffic (including voice calls, SMS, email, and web browsing) is monitored and stored forever in NSA data centers.

In 2008, in response to a high volume of litigation following from the wiretap scandal, the US Congress passed amendments to the 1978 FISA law, which were immediately signed in by the President. These created grounds for the grant of a highly controversial "retroactive immunity" against prosecution for violation of FISA. Senator Barack Obama, during

his presidential campaign, had made "transparency" a part of his platform, and promised to protect whistleblowers, but when he entered office
in 2009 his Justice Department continued the Bush administration's
policies, eventually defeating the Hepting case and others with the grant
of "retroactive immunity" for AT&T.

While the Justice Department's investigation into the source of the
original New York Times story failed to turn up the whistleblower,
it did uncover whistleblowers that had come forward after the story.
One such was Thomas Drake, a former senior executive of the NSA,
who had for years complained internally to Congressional Intelligence
Oversight Committees about corruption and wastefulness within the
NSA's "Trailblazer" program. The internal complaints were suppressed,
as were any government employees willing to pursue them. After the
New York Times story, Drake had disclosed the Trailblazer story to the
Baltimore Sun. He was indicted by a Grand Jury investigation, designated
an "enemy of the state," and charged under the Espionage Act. See "The
Secret Sharer," New Yorker, May 23, 2011: http://www.newyorker.com/
reporting/2011/05/23/110523fa_fact_mayer?currentPage=all.

The Drake prosecution collapsed after intense public scrutiny in June
2011, and after unsuccessful attempts to compel Drake into a plea bar-
gain the Justice Department settled for his plea of guilty in respect of one
minor misdemeanor. Drake received one year of probation.

The fallout from the NSA surveillance scandal continues. The ACLU is
litigating to challenge the constitutionality of the 2008 FISA amendments
in Amnesty et. al. v. Clapper. See "FISA Amendment Act Challenge,"
ACLU, September 24, 2012: http://www.aclu.org/national-security/
amnesty-et-al-v-clapper.

In Jewel v. NSA, the EFF is seeking to put an end to the NSA's warrantless surveillance. The case was dismissed in 2009 after the Obama admin-
istration argued immunity by virtue of national security secrets. See the
EFF page on Jewel v. NSA: https://www.eff.org/cases/jewel. However,
the Ninth Circuit Court of Appeals allowed the case to be reopened in
December 2011. Thomas Drake and other NSA whistleblowers William
Binney and J. Kirk Wiebe are giving evidence in Jewel v. NSA. The
Obama administration—which ran on a platform of government transparency—has prosecuted more whistleblowers under the Espionage
Act than all previous administrations combined. (All links in this note
accessed October 23, 2012.)

45.   See the entry for the Eagle system on buggedplanet:

http://buggedplanet.info/index.php?title=AMESYS#Strategic_.28.22Massive.22.29_Appliances (accessed October 22, 2012).

46. "German court orders stored telecoms data deletion," BBC, March 2, 2010: http://news.bbc.co.uk/1/hi/world/europe/8545772.stm (accessed October 15, 2012).

47. Directive 2006/24/EC of the European Parliament and Council requires European states to store citizens' telecommunications data for six to twenty-four months. It was the application of this Directive to German law that was ruled unconstitutional in Germany. In May 2012 the EU Commission referred Germany to the European Court of Justice for not complying with the Directive (see the Commission's press release: http://europa.eu/rapid/press-release_IP-12-530_en.htm (accessed October 15, 2012)).

48. See "Sweden approves wiretapping law," BBC, June 19, 2008: http://news.bbc.co.uk/1/hi/world/europe/7463333.stm.
     For more on the FRA-lagen, see Wikipedia: http://en.wikipedia.org/wiki/FRA_law (both links accessed October 10, 2012).

49. Metadata is "data about data." In the context of this discussion, metadata refers to data other than the "content" of the electronic communication. It is the front of the envelope, rather than the contents. Surveillance of metadata does not target the contents of emails, but rather all the information surrounding the contents—who the email was sent to or from, the IP addresses (and therefore location) from which it was sent, the times and dates of each email, etc. The point is, however, that the technology to intercept metadata is the same technology as the technology to intercept the contents. If you grant someone the right to surveil your metadata, their equipment must also intercept the contents of your communications. Besides this, most people do not realize that "metadata in aggregate is content"—when all the metadata is put together it provides an astonishingly detailed picture of a person's communications.

50. Amesys is part of the Bull group, once a competitor to IBM's Dehomag in selling punch card systems to the Nazis. See Edwin Black, IBM and the Holocaust (Crown Books, 2001).
     For more on how Gaddafi spied on Libyans in the UK using Amesys surveillance equipment see, "Exclusive: How Gaddafi Spied on the Fathers of the New Libya," OWNI.eu, December 1, 2011: http://owni.eu/2011/12/01/exclusive-how-gaddafi-spied-on-the-fathers-of-the-new-libya (accessed October 22, 2012).

51. WikiLeaks began releasing The Spy Files, exposing the extent of mass surveillance, in December 2011. They can be accessed at http://wikileaks.org/the-spyfiles.html.

52. For more detail see buggedplanet: http://buggedplanet.info/index.php?title=LY

53. The Chaos Communication Congress is an annual meeting of the international hacker scene, organized by the Chaos Computer Club.

54. Jacob is referring to ZTE, one of two Chinese producers (the other being Huawei) of electronic goods that are widely suspected of containing "backdoors." Jacob means to suggest that the "gift" of communications infrastructure comes with a cost—that it will, by design, be susceptible to Chinese surveillance.

55. Kill Your Television is the name for a form of protest against mass communications, whereby people eschew television for social activities.

56. The "network effect" is the effect that one person's performing an activity has on other people's likelihood to perform that activity.

57. For more on the Grand Jury investigation, see "Note on the various attempts to persecute WikiLeaks and people associated with it" preceding the discussion.

58. According to the Wall Street Journal: "The U.S. government has obtained a controversial type of secret court order to force Google Inc. and small Internet provider Sonic.net Inc. to turn over information from the email accounts of WikiLeaks volunteer Jacob Appelbaum, according to documents reviewed by The Wall Street Journal... The WikiLeaks case became a test bed for the law's interpretation earlier this year when Twitter fought a court order to turn over records from the accounts of WikiLeaks supporters including Mr. Appelbaum... The order sought the "Internet protocol," or IP, addresses of the devices from which people logged into their accounts. An IP address is a unique number assigned to a device connected to the Internet. The order also sought the email addresses of the people with whom those accounts communicated. The order was filed under seal, but Twitter successfully won from the court the right to notify the subscribers whose information was sought... The court orders reviewed by the Journal seek the same type of information that Twitter was asked to turn over. The secret Google order is dated Jan. 4 and directs the search giant to hand over the IP address from which Mr. Appelbaum logged into his gmail.com account and the email and IP addresses of the users with whom he communicated dating back to Nov. 1, 2009. It isn't clear whether Google fought the order or turned over

documents. The secret Sonic order is dated April 15 and directs Sonic to turn over the same type of information from Mr. Appelbaum's email account dating back to Nov. 1, 2009. On Aug. 31, the court agreed to lift the seal on the Sonic order to provide Mr. Appelbaum a copy of it." "Secret orders target email," Wall Street Journal, October 9, 2011: http://online.wsj.com/article/SB10001424052970203476804576613284007315072.html (accessed October 11, 2012). For more detail, see "Note on the various attempts to persecute WikiLeaks and people associated with it" preceding the discussion.

59. "WikiLeaks demands Google and Facebook unseal US subpoenas," Guardian, January 8, 2011: http://www.guardian.co.uk/media/2011/jan/08/wikileaks-calls-google-facebook-us-subpoenas (accessed October 16, 2012).
     For more detail, see "Note on the various attempts to persecute WikiLeaks and people associated with it" preceding the discussion.

60. See "Note on the various attempts to persecute WikiLeaks and people associated with it" preceding the discussion.

61. For more details see the Europe versus Facebook website: http://www.europe-v-facebook.org/EN/Data_Pool/data_pool.html (accessed October 24, 2012).

62. A National Security Letter, or NSL, is a letter from a US agency demanding "non-content data" or "metadata," such as financial transaction records, IP logs or email contacts. Anyone who receives an NSL must turn over the requested records or face prosecution. An NSL does not require authorization by a court—it can be issued directly by a federal agency. For this reason it is similar to a so-called "administrative subpoena"—an order to produce information that requires only administrative, rather than judicial, oversight. On this basis, NSLs arguably violate Fourth Amendment protections against arbitrary search and seizure. NSLs also contain a "gag component," which means that it is a criminal offense for someone who receives an NSL to talk about it to anyone else. On this basis, NSLs arguably violate First Amendment protections on the freedom of speech. In Doe v. Gonzales, the gag provision of NSLs was ruled unconstitutional. The law was changed to grant recipients of an NSL rights to challenge the NSL in court, which satisfied the Second Circuit Court that their use was no longer unconstitutional. NSLs continue to be criticized by civil liberties groups, and challenged in court. The use of NSLs vastly increased after the passage of the USA PATRIOT Act in 2001. The recipients of NSLs are typically service providers, such

as ISPs or financial institutions. The records sought are normally those of the customers of the recipient. The recipient cannot inform the customer that their records have been demanded. While recipients have rights to challenge NSLs in court, the gag provision prevents the target from even knowing about the NSL, and therefore prevents them challenging it in court. To illustrate how difficult this is to justify, see a video of the FBI's deputy general counsel attempting to answer Jacob Appelbaum's question, "How am I supposed to go to a judge if the third party is gagged from telling me that I'm targeted by you?" Her answer, "There are times when we have to have those things in place," is chilling: http://youtu.be/dTuxoLDnmJU (also found with further contextual material at Privacy SOS: http://privacysos.org/node/727).

According to the Electronic Frontier Foundation, "Of all the dangerous government surveillance powers that were expanded by the USA PATRIOT Act the National Security Letter (NSL) power under 18 U.S.C. § 2709 as expanded by PATRIOT Section 505 is one of the most frightening and invasive. These letters served on communications service providers like phone companies and ISPs allow the FBI to secretly demand data about ordinary American citizens' private communications and Internet activity without any meaningful oversight or prior judicial review. Recipients of NSLs are subject to a gag order that forbids them from ever revealing the letters' existence to their coworkers, to their friends or even to their family members, much less the public." See: https://www.eff.org/issues/national-security-letters. See also the Electronic Frontier Foundation's collection of documents relating to National Security Letters released under the Freedom of Information Act: https://www.eff.org/issues/foia/07656JDB (all links in this note accessed October 23, 2012).

63. See note 41 above on the "First Crypto Wars" of the 1990s.
64. Julian is referring to SSL/TLS, which is a cryptographic protocol now incorporated as standard into all web browsers, and used for secure browsing—for example, whenever a browser is used for internet banking.
65. For one example among many, see, "Blackberry, Twitter probed in London riots," Bloomberg, August 9, 2011: http://www.bloomberg.com/news/2011-08-09/blackberry-messages-probed-in-u-k-rioting-as-police-say-looting-organized.html (accessed October 16, 2012).
66. For example, a member of the LulzSec group that exposed flaws in Sony's security practices by releasing Sony customers' personal data was arrested after his identity was gained from the proxy site HideMyAss.

com, via a court order in the US. See, "Lulzsec hacker pleads guilty over Sony attack," BBC, October 15, 2012: http://www.bbc.com/news/technology-19949624 (accessed October 15, 2012).

67. SOPA refers to the Stop Online Piracy Act. PIPA refers to the Protect Intellectual Property Act. Both are proposed US laws which came to world prominence in early 2012. Both are transparent legislative expressions of the desire of the content industry, represented by bodies like the Recording Industry Association of America, to enforce intellectual property law globally, and as heavily as possible, in response to the free distribution of cultural artifacts online. Both laws proposed to grant heavy-handed and wide-reaching internet censorship powers to US law enforcement agencies, which threatened to "break the internet." Both laws earned the ire of substantial portions of the international online community and provoked a strong reaction from the industrial actors whose interests are in a free and open internet.

In early 2012, Reddit, Wikipedia and several thousand other sites blacked out their services in protest against the laws, instigating heavy public pressure on public representatives. Other online service providers, such as Google, encouraged petitions. In response, both laws were suspended, pending reconsideration and discussion of whether they represent the best approach to the problem of intellectual property online. The episode is seen as the first significant discovery and assertion of effective congressional lobbying power by the internet industry.

68. See the "Note on the various attempts to persecute WikiLeaks and people associated with it" preceding the discussion.

69. ACTA refers to the Anti-Counterfeit and Trade Agreement. It is a multilateral international treaty negotiated in secret over the course of years, led by the United States and Japan, part of which institutes new and draconian obligations to protect intellectual property.

Initial drafts of ACTA were revealed to the public in 2008 after they were leaked to WikiLeaks, provoking widespread outcry from free culture activists and online advocates. See the ACTA section on WikiLeaks: http://wikileaks.org/wiki/Category:ACTA.

US diplomatic cables shared with La Quadrature Du Net by WikiLeaks in early 2011 showed that ACTA was negotiated in secret explicitly in order to fast track the creation of extreme IP enforcement rules, which could later be coercively imposed on poorer countries excluded from the agreement. See, "WikiLeaks Cables Shine Light on ACTA History," La

Quadrature Du Net, February 3, 2011: http://www.laquadrature.net/en/wikileaks-cables-shine-light-on-acta-history (accessed October 23, 2012). In July 2012, after a campaign led by La Quadrature Du Net and Jérémie Zimmermann, ACTA was defeated in the European Parliament.

70. M.A.I.D., (Mutually) Assured Information Destruction, is "a framework that provides time sensitive remote key escrow and provable authentication with optional distress coding. It automatically destroys cryptographic keys after a given user configurable time threshold is crossed": https://www.noisebridge.net/wiki/M.A.I.D.

Legislation such as the Regulation of Investigatory Powers Act of 2000, or RIPA, makes the United Kingdom quite a hostile regime for cryptography. Under RIPA individuals can be obliged to decrypt data or surrender a password on the order of a police constable. No judicial oversight is necessary. Refusal to comply can result in criminal charges. In a resulting trial, if the defendant claims she/he has forgotten the password, there is a reverse burden of proof. In order to avoid being convicted the defendant must prove that she/he has forgotten the password. This, it is argued by critics of the law, effectuates a presumption of guilt. Comparatively, while there has been much litigation in connection with the same issues in the United States, and the situation is by no means ideal, there has been far more success invoking the First and Fourth Amendments in similar circumstances. See the report, "Freedom from Suspicion, Surveillance Reform for a Digital Age," published by JUSTICE, November 4, 2011, available from: http://www.justice.org.uk/resources.php/305/freedom-from-suspicion.

For more on the Rubberhose file system, see, "The Idiot Savants' Guide to Rubberhose," Suelette Dreyfus: http://marutukku.org/current/src/doc/maruguide/t1.html (all links accessed October 24, 2012).

71. An archive of the old Cypherpunk mailing list can be downloaded from: http://cryptome.org/cpunks/cpunks-92-98.zip.

Tim May was a founding member of the Cypherpunks mailing list. See his Cyphernomicon, an FAQ on cypherpunk history and philosophy: http://www.cypherpunks.to/faq/cyphernomicron/cyphernomicon.html (both links accessed October 24, 2012).

72. "Proposed US ACTA plurilateral intellectual property trade agreement (2007)," WikiLeaks, May 22, 2008: http://wikileaks.org/wiki/Proposed_US_ACTA_multi-lateral_intellectual_property_trade_agreement_%282007%29 (accessed October 21, 2012).

73. "Massive Takedown of Anti-Scientology Videos on YouTube," Electronic Frontier Foundation, September 5, 2008: https://www.eff.org/deep-links/2008/09/massive-takedown-anti-scientology-videos-youtube (accessed October 16, 2012).

74. "EU-India Free Trade Agreement draft, 24 Feb 2009," WikiLeaks, June 23, 2009: http://wikileaks.org/wiki/EU-India_Free_Trade_Agreement_draft,_24_Feb_2009 (accessed October 21, 2012).

75. Peer-to-peer, or P2P, refers to a network in which each computer can act as a client or a server for all the others (each computer can both give and receive information), allowing for the rapid sharing of content such as music, videos, documents or any kind of digital information.

76. Cloud computing refers to a situation where many of the functions traditionally performed by a computer, such as storing data (including user data for various applications), hosting and running software, and providing the processing power to run the software, is done remotely, outside of the computer itself, "in the cloud"—generally by companies offering cloud computing services via the internet. Rather than needing a full personal computer anymore, all the user needs is a device that can access the internet, and the rest is served to the user over the internet. The metaphor "in the cloud" obscures the fact that all the user's data and metadata are actually on a remote computer somewhere in a data center, most likely controlled by a big company such as Amazon, and while users no longer have complete control over it, someone else does.

77. See the "Note on the various attempts to persecute WikiLeaks and people associated with it" preceding the discussion.

78. DIASPORA is a social network that allows each user to act as their own server by installing the DIASPORA software, enabling them to retain control of their own data. It was created as a privacy-compliant alternative to Facebook. It is non-profit and user-owned: http://diasporaproject.org

79. The original Napster (1999-2001) was a pioneering peer-to-peer service for sharing music. It was enormously popular but was soon shut down by legal action over copyright infringement from the Recording Industry Association of America. After bankruptcy the name Napster was bought and used for a separate online store selling music for money.

80. See the "Note on the various attempts to persecute WikiLeaks and people associated with it" preceding the discussion.

81. Benjamin Bayart is president of the French Data Network, the oldest active ISP in France, and an advocate of net neutrality and free

software. See his Wikipedia entry (in French): http://fr.wikipedia.org/wiki/Benjamin_Bayart (accessed October 15, 2012).

82. Larry Lessig is an American academic and activist best known for his views on copyright and free culture. He blogs at: http://lessig.tumblr.com (accessed October 15, 2012).

83. There is plenty of fascinating content in the US diplomatic cables released by WikiLeaks on this issue. For some interesting discussion, consult the following cables (by cable reference ID, links all accessed October 24, 2012):

07BEIRUT1301: http://wikileaks.org/cable/2007/08/07BEIRUT1301.html
08BEIRUT490: http://wikileaks.org/cable/2008/04/08BEIRUT490.html
08BEIRUT505: http://wikileaks.org/cable/2008/04/08BEIRUT505.html
08BEIRUT523: http://wikileaks.org/cable/2008/04/08BEIRUT523.html

84. See cable reference ID 10MOSCOW228, WikiLeaks: http://wikileaks.org/cable/2010/02/10MOSCOW228.html (accessed October 24, 2012).

85. For more on the due-process-free killing of American citizens Anwar al-Awlaki and his son Abdulrahman al-Awlaki see Glenn Greenwald, "The due-process-free assassination of U.S. citizens is now reality," Salon, September 30, 2011: http://www.salon.com/2011/09/30/awlaki_6. And "The killing of Awlaki's 16-year-old son," Salon, October 20, 2011: http://www.salon.com/2011/10/20/the_killing_of_awlakis_16_year_old_son.

"It is literally impossible to imagine a more violent repudiation of the basic blueprint of the republic than the development of a secretive, totally unaccountable executive branch agency that simultaneously collects information about all citizens and then applies a "disposition matrix" to determine what punishment should be meted out. This is classic political dystopia brought to reality"—Glenn Greenwald, "Obama moves to make the War on Terror permanent," Guardian, October 24, 2012: http://www.guardian.co.uk/commentisfree/2012/oct/24/obama-terrorism-kill-list (all links accessed October 24, 2012).

86. For further information please consult The Anonymity Bibliography, Selected Papers in Anonymity, curated by Roger Dingledine and Nick Mathewson: http://freehaven.net/anonbib (accessed October 24, 2012).

Chaumian currencies are centrally issued, but use cryptography to ensure anonymous transactions. Chaumian currencies contrast with Bitcoin, another electronic currency discussed extensively below, where all transactions are public but the currency has no central authority.

87. For more on the banking blockade of WikiLeaks see the "Note on the various attempts to persecute WikiLeaks and people associated with it" preceding the discussion.

88. Julian is here referring to UK government plans to increase the use of electronic tags. See, "Over 100,000 offenders to be electronically tagged," Guardian, March 25, 2012: http://www.guardian.co.uk/society/2012/mar/25/prisons-and-probation-criminal-justice (accessed October 22, 2012).

    At the time of the discussion Julian was under house arrest pending the outcome of his extradition case. After his solitary confinement without charge in December 2010, Julian's detention was converted to house arrest after providing bail moneys of over £300,000. As a condition of his bail he was confined to a specified address between certain hours, and this regime was enforced by an electronic tag fixed to his ankle, operated by a private security firm on contract to the UK government. Julian's movements were controlled to the extent that he was compelled to check in with the police daily, by a particular time, for over 550 days. At the time of publication, Julian is confined to the Ecuadorian embassy in London, which is surrounded at all times by the London Metropolitan Police. In June 2012 Julian entered the embassy seeking political asylum from persecution by the United States government and its allies. He received asylum in August 2012.

89. "Is CCA Trying to Take Over the World?" American Civil Liberties Union, February 21, 2012: http://www.aclu.org/blog/prisoners-rights/cca-trying-take-over-world.

    "Passing House Bill will worsen already pressing civil rights issue," ANNARBOR.com, August 2, 2012: http://annarbor.com/news/opinion/passing-house-bill-will-worsen-already-pressing-civil-rights-issue.

    See also "Goldman Sachs to invest $9.6m in New York inmate rehabilitation," Guardian, August 2, 2012: http://www.guardian.co.uk/society/2012/aug/02/goldman-sachs-invest-new-york-jail (all links accessed October 24, 2012).

90. Bitcoin (http://bitcoin.org) is the first truly successful implementation of a classic cypherpunk concept: the cryptographic digital currency. Bitcoin is discussed extensively below, but an excellent introductory explanation on the technology and philosophy behind it can be found in, "Understanding Bitcoin," Al Jazeera, June 9, 2012: http://www.aljazeera.com/indepth/opinion/2012/05/20125309437931677.html (accessed October 22, 2012).

91. e-gold was a digital currency and business started in 1996. The owners and proprietors were indicted by the US Department of Justice for "conspiracy to engage in money laundering." They pleaded guilty, and were given sentences of probation, home detention and community services. The sentencing judge claimed they deserved lenient sentences because they had not intended to engage in illegal activity. See, "Bullion and Bandits: The Improbable Rise and Fall of E-Gold," Wired, June 9, 2009: http://www.wired.com/threatlevel/2009/06/e-gold (accessed October 22, 2012).

92. Before the Internet, the X.25 network was the major global network for data exchange existing in parallel to the telephone network. The billing on X.25 was based on the amount of data sent and received, not on the length of a connection as with the telephone network. Gateways (so called PADs) allowed connection to the X.25 network from the telephone network with modems or acoustic couplers. For more details see Wikipedia: http://en.wikipedia.org/wiki/X.25 (accessed October 24, 2012).

93. David Chaum is a cryptographer and inventor of cryptographic protocols. He is a pioneer of digital currency technologies and introduced eCash, one of the first anonymous cryptographic electronic currencies.

94. On the effect of the negative press see, "Bitcoin implodes, falls more than 90 percent from June peak," arstechnica, October 18, 2011: http://arstechnica.com/tech-policy/2011/10/bitcoin-implodes-down-more-than-90-percent-from-june-peak (accessed October 22, 2012).

95. See, for example, "The Underground Website Where You Can Buy Any Drug Imaginable," Gawker, June 1, 2011: http://gawker.com/5805928/the-underground-website-where-you-can-buy-any-drug-imaginable (accessed October 22, 2012).

96. Lawrence Lessig's early work on copyright and culture (for example in his book Free Culture (2004)) has been supplanted in recent years by an interest in the corruption of American democracy through congressional lobbying. See The Lessig Wiki: http://wiki.lessig.org

97. The California Correctional Peace Officers Association is an influential special interest group in California that routinely donates seven-figure totals in state elections, although it is not, year for year, the single largest campaign donor. See "California reelin," The Economist, March 17, 2011: http://www.economist.com/node/18359882. And "The Golden State's Iron Bars," Reason, July 2011: http://reason.com/archives/2011/06/23/the-golden-states-iron-bars. See also the California Correctional Peace Officers Association entry on the FollowThe

Money website of the National Institute for Money in State Politics: http://www.followthemoney.org/database/topcontributor.phtml?u=3286&y=0 (all links accessed October 22, 2012).

98. Heinz von Foerster (1911-2002) was an Austrian-American scientist and an architect of cybernetics. His so-called "ethical imperative" or common motto is: "Act always so as to increase the number of choices," or in German, "Handle stets so, daß die Anzahl der Wahlmöglichkeiten größer wird."

99. Jacob attributes this observation to John Gilmore.

100. For more on the harassment of Jacob and other people associated with WikiLeaks see the "Note on the various attempts to persecute WikiLeaks and people associated with it" preceding the discussion.

101. Isaac Mao is a Chinese blogger, software architect and venture capitalist. He is a co-founder of CNBlog.org and board member to the Tor Project.

102. See the WikiLeaks page on Nadhmi Auchi: http://wikileaks.org/wiki/Nadhmi_Auchi (accessed October 24, 2012).

103. The stories can be found at WikiLeaks here: http://wikileaks.org/wiki/Eight_stories_on_Obama_linked_billionaire_Nadhmi_Auchi_censored_from_the_Guardian,_Observer,_Telegraph_and_New_Statesman (accessed October 24, 2012).

104. As a general note both http://cables.mrkva.eu/ and http://cablegatesearch.net provide excellent ways of comparing redacted versions of cables with full versions, in order to see what WikiLeaks' media partners redacted.

105. "Qaddafi's Son Is Bisexual and Other Things the New York Times Doesn't Want You to Know," Gawker, September 16, 2011: http://gawker.com/5840809/qaddafis-son-is-bisexual-and-other-things-the-new-york-times-doesnt-want-you-to-know-about.
The specific example cited refers to cable reference ID 06TRIPOLI198, WikiLeaks: https://wikileaks.org/cable/2006/05/06TRIPOLI198.html.
The redactions can be seen visually on the Cablegatesearch website which shows the revision history, with the redactions shaded in pink: http://www.cablegatesearch.net/cable.php?id=06TRIPOLI198&version=1291757400 (all links accessed October 22, 2012).

106. For the original cable see cable reference ID 10STATE17263, WikiLeaks: http://wikileaks.org/cable/2010/02/10STATE17263.html.
For the New York Times story see, "Iran Fortifies Its Arsenal With the Aid of North Korea," New York Times, November 29, 2010: http://www.nytimes.com/2010/11/29/world/middleeast/29missiles.html?_r=0.

The same cable was also used by David Leigh of the Guardian for his story, "WikiLeaks cables expose Pakistan nuclear fears," Guardian, November 30, 2010: http://www.guardian.co.uk/world/2010/nov/30/wikileaks-cables-pakistan-nuclear-fears. The redacted version of the cable published by the Guardian, without a cable reference number, reduced it to just two paragraphs relating to Pakistan. "US embassy cables: XXXXXXXXXXXXX," Guardian, November 30, 2010: http://www.guardian.co.uk/world/us-embassy-cables-documents/250573.

The extent of the redaction can be seen visually on the Cablegatesearch website which shows the revision history, with the redaction of nearly the whole document shaded in pink: http://www.cablegatesearch.net/cable.php?id=10STATE17263&version=1291486260 (all links accessed October 22, 2012).

107. For the original cable see cable reference ID 08KYIV2414, WikiLeaks: http://wikileaks.org/cable/2008/12/08KYIV2414.html.

For the Guardian redacted version see, "US embassy cables: Gas supplies linked to Russian mafia," December 1, 2010: http://www.guardian.co.uk/world/us-embassy-cables-documents/182121?INTCMP=SRCH.

The redaction can be seen visually on the Cablegatesearch website which shows the revision history, with the redactions shaded in pink: http://www.cablegatesearch.net/cable.php?id=08KYIV2414&version=1291255260 (all links accessed October 22, 2012).

108. For the original cable see cable reference ID 10ASTANA72, WikiLeaks: http://wikileaks.org/cable/2010/01/10ASTANA72.html.

For the Guardian redacted version see, "US embassy cables: Kazakhstan - the big four," Guardian, November 29, 2010: http://www.guardian.co.uk/world/us-embassy-cables-documents/245167?INTCMP=SRCH.

The redaction can be seen visually on the Cablegatesearch website which shows the revision history, with the redactions shaded in pink: http://www.cablegatesearch.net/cable.php?id=10ASTANA72&version=1291113360 (all links accessed October 22, 2012).

109. See, for example, cable reference ID 09TRIPOLI413 about Western energy companies operating in Libya. The visual representation on the Cablegatesearch website, with the Guardian's redactions shaded in pink, shows that the Guardian removed all references to the names of energy companies and their executives, except for references to Russian energy company Gazprom. Even though some of the content is somewhat mitigating for the Western companies, the redactions are elaborate, and the redacted version gives quite a different picture:

http://www.cablegatesearch.net/cable.php?id=09TRIPOLI413&version=1296509820 (accessed October 22, 2012).

110. In this example the original cable contained 5,226 words. The redacted version published by the Guardian had only 1,406 words.

For the original cable see cable reference ID 05SOFIA1207, WikiLeaks: http://wikileaks.org/cable/2005/07/05SOFIA1207.html.

For the Guardian redacted version see, "US embassy cables: Organised crime in Bulgaria," December 1, 2010: http://www.guardian.co.uk/world/us-embassy-cables-documents/36013.

For the Guardian news story based on the cable see, "WikiLeaks cables: Russian government "using mafia for its dirty work"," Guardian, December 1, 2010: http://www.guardian.co.uk/world/2010/dec/01/wikileaks-cable-spain-russian-mafia.

The extent of the redaction can be seen visually on the Cablegatesearch website which shows the revision history, with the redactions shaded in pink: http://www.cablegatesearch.net/cable.php?id=05SOFIA1207&version=1291757400.

This Bulgarian example is discussed by WikiLeaks' Bulgarian media partner Bivol in, "Unedited cable from Sofia shows the total invasion of the state by organized crime (Update: Cable Comparison)," WL Central, March 18, 2011: http://wlcentral.org/node/1480. In addition see, "The Guardian: Redacting, censoring or lying?" WL Central, March 19, 2012: http://wlcentral.org/node/1490. Also of note below both WL Central stories is the comment from Guardian journalist David Leigh and the responses (all links accessed October 22, 2012).

111. This refers to cable reference ID 09BERLIN1108. The redactions can be seen visually on the Cablegatesearch website which shows the revision history, with the redactions shaded in pink: http://www.cablegatesearch.net/cable.php?id=09BERLIN1108&version=1291380660 (accessed October 22, 2012).

112. For more examples, see the cabledrum website: www.cabledrum.net/pages/censorship.php

113. "Interception of telecommunications. The Presidency provided information on the state of play... It recalled the negative press that this issue has received in the media... Against this background, the Presidency thus recognized that progress in this matter is being very slow... Several delegations expressed some caution as regards the preparation of a press release, noting that this could provoke a chain reaction and further negative press in the media. The Commission, whilst noting that its position has not changed, informed delegations that a possible way to break the

deadlock could be following a similar strategy as that followed in tackling the issue of child pornography in the Internet. Although acknowledging that this was a different topic it also has an interception dimension"— European Commission, Police Co-operation Working Group meeting on interception of telecommunications, October 13-14, 1999. Full document at: http://www.quintessenz.at/doqs/000100002292/1999_10_13,Police%20Cooperation%20Working%20Group%20mixed%20committee%20meeting.pdf (accessed October 24, 2012).

114. See the "Note on the various attempts to persecute WikiLeaks and people associated with it" preceding the discussion.

115. Jacob is referring to Gilmore v. Gonzales, 435 F.3d 1125 (9th Cir. 2006). John Gilmore, an original cypherpunk, took a case as far as the US Supreme Court to disclose the contents of a secret law—a Security Directive—restricting citizens' rights to travel on an airplane without identification. Besides challenging the constitutionality of such a provision, Gilmore was challenging the fact that the provision itself was secret and could not be disclosed, even though it has binding effects on US citizens. The court consulted the Security Directive in camera, and ruled against Gilmore on the Directive's constitutionality. The contents of the law were, however, never disclosed during the course of the proceedings. See Gilmore v Gonzales at PapersPlease.org: http://papersplease.org/gilmore/facts.html (accessed October 22, 2012).

116. Christiania is a self-declared self-governing area in Copenhagen, Denmark. A former military barracks, it was occupied in the 1970s by a broadly collectivist/anarchist community. It has carved out a unique legal status in Denmark.

117. The principle of "net neutrality" (short for network neutrality) requires ISPs to be prevented (by law, it is usually argued) from restricting their users' access to networks that participate in the internet, including restricting content. See the Electronic Frontier Foundation's page on net neutrality: https://www.eff.org/issues/net-neutrality (accessed October 24, 2012).

118. "Blocking WikiLeaks emails trips up Bradley Manning prosecution," Politico, March 15, 2012: http://www.politico.com/blogs/under-the-radar/2012/03/blocking-wikileaks-emails-trips-up-bradley-manning-117573.html (accessed October 21, 2012).

119. For more information on Wau Holland see the Wau Holland Stiftung: http://www.wauland.de

120. "Stasi still in charge of Stasi files," WikiLeaks, October 4, 2007: http://www.wikileaks.org/wiki/Stasi_still_in_charge_of_Stasi_files (accessed October 22, 2012).

121. "Here's what you can do to change the world, right now, to a better ride. Take all that money that we spend on weapons and defense each year, and instead spend it feeding, clothing and educating the poor of the world, which it would many times over, not one human being excluded, and we could explore space, together, both inner and outer, forever, in peace"—Bill Hicks. For a video of the line being performed see, "Bill Hicks—Positive Drugs Story": http://youtu.be/vX1CvW38cHA (accessed October 24, 2012).

122. The Sarbanes-Oxley Act of 2002 is a US law passed in reaction to the corporate and accounting scandals of Enron, Tyco International, Adelphia, Peregrine Systems and WorldCom. The Act aimed to eliminate the same corrupt practices that had led to these crises. Section 1107 of the Act, codified as USC 1513(e), creates a criminal offense over attempts to retaliate against whistleblowers.

123. Evgeny Morozov, The Net Delusion: The Dark Side of Internet Freedom (Public Affairs, 2011).

124. On free software see, "The Free Software Definition," from the website of the GNU Operating System: https://www.gnu.org/philosophy/free-sw.html.

    Free hardware means hardware that is not encumbered by proprietary patents, that is constructed to open standards, where there are no laws against reverse engineering or tampering (no anti-circumvention laws), and where the design principles, instructions and plans are made freely available so that anyone else who has them and the necessary resources can build a replica.

    For more on free hardware see, "Exceptionally Hard and Soft Meeting: exploring the frontiers of open source and DIY," EHSM: http://ehsm.eu. See also, "Open-source hardware" on Wikipedia: https://en.wikipedia.org/wiki/Open-source_hardware (all links accessed October 24, 2012).

125. On 3D printing using free and open hardware see an introductory video to the RepRap 3D printer: http://vimeo.com/5202148 (accessed October 24, 2012).

126. "Be the trouble you want to see in the world," is taken from A Softer World, a photographic webcomic: http://www.asofterworld.com/index.php?id=189 (accessed October 24, 2012).

127. To follow up on any of the issues raised in the discussion, Jacob recom-
     mends the following two bibliographic resources:
     The Anonymity Bibliography, Selected Papers in Anonymity, curated by
     Roger Dingledine and Nick Mathewson: http://freehaven.net/anonbib
     The Censorship Bibliography, Selected Papers in Censorship, curated by
     Philipp Winter: www.cs.kau.se/philwint/censorbib (both links accessed
     October 24, 2012).

128. Footnote left intentionally blank.

129. Nawaat.org is an independent collective blog in Tunisia launched in 2004:
     http://nawaat.org/portail.
     Tunileaks was launched by Nawaat in November 2010, publishing cables
     from WikiLeaks related to Tunisia: https://tunileaks.appspot.com.
     For more on Tunilinks and the Ben-Ali government's censorship efforts
     against it see, "Tunisia: Censorship Continues as Wikileaks Cables
     Make the Rounds," Global Voices Advocacy, December 7, 2010: http://
     advocacy.globalvoicesonline.org/2010/12/07/tunisia-censorship-continues-
     as-wikileaks-cables-make-the-rounds (all links accessed October 24, 2012).

The Passion of Bradley Manning
THE STORY OF THE SUSPECT BEHIND THE
LARGEST SECURITY BREACH IN U.S. HISTORY

Chase Madar

ISBN 978-1-935928-53-9 PAPERBACK
ISBN 978-1-935928-54-6 E-BOOK
190 PAGES

"Author and lawyer Chase Madar tells a great story that raises critical questions about the appropriate balance of government secrecy and national security in a modern democracy."
—Anthony D. Romero, Executive Director, American Civil Liberties Union

"The mistreatment, trial, and fate of Private Bradley Manning will undoubtedly read like an obituary on the Obama years. His case is a crucial one. Essayist and lawyer Chase Madar turned his sharp eye on it early. His will be the single must-read book on the case."
—Tom Engelhardt, TomDispatch.com

OR Books
www.orbooks.com